EXTRAORDINARY HEROES

IMPERIAL WAR
MUSEUM

FOREWORD BY LORD ASHCROFT, KCMG

First published in Great Britain in 2010 by Osprey Publishing,
Midland House, West Way, Botley, Oxford, OX2 0PH, UK
44-02 23rd Street, Suite 219, Long Island City, NY 11101, USA
E-mail: info@ospreypublishing.com

A CIP catalogue record for this book is available from the British Library
ISBN: 978 1 84908 389 8

Page layout by Ken Vail Graphic Design, Cambridge, UK
Typeset in Perpetua
Originated by PPS Grasmere Ltd, Leeds, UK
Printed in China through Worldprint

10 11 12 13 14   10 9 8 7 6 5 4 3 2 1

Images on page 3, left to right: Kamal Ram (IWM, ART LD 4516); Wooden cross from Noel Chavasse's grave (IWM, LI 2009 999 162 31); Francis Maxwell (IWM, VC 806); Charles Gough in action (National Army Museum); Matthew Croucher (Topfoto); HMS *Dunraven* in action (IWM, ART 5130); Daphne Pearson (IWM, ART LD 626)
Portrait of Lord Ashcroft on page 4: Photograph Jon Enoch/Eyevine
Portrait of Nigel Steel on page 5: IWM 2010 019 036

Osprey Publishing is supporting the Woodland Trust, the UK's leading woodland conservation charity, by funding the dedication of trees.

www.ospreypublishing.com

IMPERIAL WAR MUSEUM COLLECTIONS
Many of the photos in this book come from the Imperial War Museum's huge collections which cover all aspects of conflict involving Britain and the Commonwealth since the start of the twentieth century. These rich resources are available online to search, browse and buy at www.iwmcollections.org.uk. In addition to Collections Online, you can visit the Visitor Rooms where you can explore over 8 million photographs, thousands of hours of moving images, the largest sound archive of its kind in the world, thousands of diaries and letters written by people in wartime, and a huge reference library. To make an appointment, call (020) 7416 5320, or e-mail mail@iwm.org.uk.

Imperial War Museum
www.iwm.org.uk

AUTHOR'S NOTE
Dedicated to C.G.H.S.

I should like to thank Nigel Steel, Kate Clements, Keeley Jopson and Robert Campbell at the IWM for their help, and Emily Holmes and Kate Moore at Osprey Publishing for their support.
By dint of its size, this book can only provide a mere glimpse into the often fascinating lives of these heroic men, women and children, but I hope that readers will be tempted into reading some of the many very good books on both the history and recipients of the VC and GC.
In the main body of the book the recipients' names are given as at the time of their action, it is indicated whether they received the Victoria Cross or George Cross, and the date(s) of their action is given. Ranks, other decorations, and later name changes are not indicated. The appendix gives a full listing of medal groups in the Lord Ashcroft Gallery, and includes the rank at time of action, unit, and year and place of action.

CONTENTS

FOREWORD Michael Ashcroft

THE **IMPERIAL WAR MUSEUM'S** new Lord Ashcroft Gallery is the culmination of my lifelong fascination with a single subject: bravery. From the age of about twelve, I found myself in awe of people who had performed heroic acts in the face of terrifying threats. I looked up to those who were prepared to risk the greatest gift of all – life itself – for their comrades and their country. My late father, Eric Ashcroft, was a modest man but his own recollections of his involvement, as a young officer, in the D-Day landings at Sword Beach only served to fuel my interest in the concept of courage.

As a teenager, I had heard of something called the Victoria Cross (VC), which was only awarded in cases of truly exceptional bravery. The more I read about the VC, the more interested I became in the medal and its recipients. As a schoolboy, I had a dream that one day I might own a VC – the tangible relic of a supreme act of courage. At the age of 40, and by then having enjoyed some success as an entrepreneur, I achieved that ambition when I was the successful bidder at the auction of the VC awarded to Leading Seaman James Magennis at the end of the Second World War.

At the time, I intended the purchase to be a one-off but I soon decided that I wanted to build up a collection of Britain's foremost award for valour. Today the Lord Ashcroft Collection has more than 160 VCs – well in excess of a tenth of all such medals that have been awarded since 1856. The collection, which is held in a trust, has been amassed sensitively and responsibly. From the day when I bought my first VC at Sotheby's in July 1986, rule number one was that I only purchased medals that the owners were seeking to sell.

The collection of VCs has, quite simply, become my pride and joy – and one thing led to another. In 2006, to mark the 150th anniversary of the creation of the VC, I wrote my first book on bravery. *Victoria Cross Heroes* was an unexpected best-seller and since then I have written two further books on heroism – the most recent being *George Cross Heroes*. I have also given talks on bravery, including addressing the Cheltenham Literary Festival.

Some time ago, the trust – with my blessing – expressed a private desire to open the Lord Ashcroft Collection to the public for the first time so that the medals, and their accompanying memorabilia, could be enjoyed by others. After lengthy discussions, I was delighted that an agreement was reached to collaborate with the Imperial War Museum, which already had its own prestigious collection of VCs and GCs. The result has been the opening of the Lord Ashcroft Gallery – and, as a direct spin-off, this splendid book. I believe that the bravery and gallantry of servicemen and civilians must be cherished and celebrated. This book does just that and I invite everyone to join me in acclaiming the actions of a special group of people who have every right to be called 'the bravest of the brave'.

INTRODUCTION Nigel Steel

BRAVERY IN THE LORD ASHCROFT GALLERY

This book tells the stories of 80 remarkable people. All of them were awarded either the Victoria Cross or the George Cross – the highest recognition that Britain and the Commonwealth can give of extreme bravery. The Victoria Cross, or VC, is given for acts of great courage in the heat of battle under fierce enemy fire. The George Cross, or GC, recognises acts of equal gallantry that are carried out both in war away from the intensity of battle and in peacetime, often totally unrelated to war. The simple letters VC and GC bring immediate respect and admiration, and stand above all other honours and decorations. Why this should be so is made abundantly clear by the stories told here.

All of them are taken from the Imperial War Museum's Lord Ashcroft Gallery which was opened in November 2010 to display the VCs and GCs from the combined collections of Lord Ashcroft and the Imperial War Museum. The Lord Ashcroft Collection holds more than 160 VCs and forms the world's largest single collection. It spans the whole history of the award and highlights many aspects of the way in which the VC has developed since its inception in 1856. It contains the second ever VC, VCs awarded in all of Britain's major military engagements from the Crimea to the Falklands, VCs awarded to all three services including the first ever air VC, the first and last VCs of the twentieth century, the first VC for an action above Britain and two of the five

awarded to civilians. The collection contains something for everyone interested not just in the VC but in the highest forms of human endeavour.

Although the Lord Ashcroft Collection forms the core of the new gallery, it is framed by the existing medals held by the Imperial War Museum. In addition to nearly 50 VCs, the IWM also has almost 30 GCs. Although the George Cross was not established until 1940, it absorbed other bravery awards such as the Empire Gallantry Medal, Albert Medal and Edward Medal which had been in place for much longer. As a result the earliest 'GC' action in the gallery dates from 1916. With its wider scope, the GC has also been awarded to many women and children, as well as civilian organisations such as the police force. All of these are represented in the Lord Ashcroft Gallery and reflected in the stories of this book.

Combined the two collections offer a stark insight into human behaviour in the face of adversity. The new displays also try to be much more than simply a medal gallery. The principal interest of the medals lies not in what they are, but what they represent. They are ciphers for an underlying wealth of personalities, events and stories, each one of which is extraordinary. The medals document real human experience. Each medal group is a biography. They show where people went and what they did. By exploring them, we delve into the history of the last one and a half centuries. Each recipient was different. Some thrived under the pressure of being a VC or

GC; others were overwhelmed. Some rose from humble beginnings to great things; others returned to quiet obscurity.

To make sense of these disparate and diverse elements the Lord Ashcroft Gallery groups the medals into seven broad areas each representing a different 'quality' of bravery, namely: boldness, aggression, leadership, skill, sacrifice, initiative and endurance, and the same pattern has been used for this book. When recommending someone for either a VC or a GC a formal citation is written to record what they did and why it was so special. Each act is clearly extremely brave. But close reading of the 250 or so citations from the gallery shows a number of similarities between the actions. Although they often took place many years apart, people appear to act in timeless fashion. A number of fundamental qualities of human bravery emerge. These have been used to draw the actions together, highlighting the perceived links between them.

From these seven qualities, questions arise about the nature of bravery itself. Why do people do it? Why can some people act, when others cannot? Above all, what is bravery? There are no set answers to any of these questions. But the stories in the Lord Ashcroft Gallery, and those told in this book, allow us to consider what they might be. They offer us a chance to examine more closely the nature of bravery and the extraordinary personalities of those who have received the Victoria Cross and the George Cross.

Nigel Steel
Principal Historian
Lord Ashcroft Gallery
Imperial War Museum

BOLDNESS

'cool intrepidity and characteristic daring'

Boldness combines force with creative thinking. It is impetuous and the act is often completed before anyone knows what is going on. At certain times people take a calculated risk. With audacity, dash and daring, much can be achieved. In simple terms, 'who dares wins'.

GODFREY PLACE VC

22 September 1943

Godfrey Place (1921–94). (IWM, A 21799)

The massive German battleship *Tirpitz* rarely left her heavily defended anchorage in the fjords of Norway, but her very existence was a constant threat to Allied navies throughout the Second World War. Many attacks were made against her, but the first to do serious damage was Operation *Source*, when three midget submarines attacked the *Tirpitz*. At just 15m long, the X-craft were tiny, cramped submarines, designed to creep under target ships at anchor and deposit large explosive charges that detonated on timer fuses.

Place and the crew of the *X-7* before the raid on the *Tirpitz*. The other three men may are believed to be the passage crew, one of whom was James Magennis, who later became a VC himself, (see pp.14–15). (IWM, A 19636)

Basil Charles Godfrey Place, 22, commanded one of the tiny submarines in the raid. Born in Worcestershire in 1921, he joined the Navy as a young teenager. He was one of the early X-craft volunteers in November 1942, commanding an experimental X-craft before taking command of the operational *X-7*. Two officers and an engine room artificer completed the crew of the submarine.

Before he even reached the fjord, Place had to take *X-7* through miles of minefields. After recharging the batteries of the submarine on the surface, Place dived in the early Scandinavian dawn on 22 September, ready to battle through the series of underwater nets that protected the battleship. Place found a gap in the outer net, but then got tangled in the next. It took an hour of struggling before he finally broke through. Place could now see the *Tirpitz* just a mile away. But before they could get close, they had to force their way through yet another net.

Meanwhile one of the other submarines attacking the *Tirpitz* had been sighted. The commander of the *X-6*, Lieutenant Cameron, managed to release his charges before scuttling the craft. The Germans now knew an attack was underway.

Finally *X-7* broke through the net, and surfaced just 30 yards from the battleship. At full speed the *X-7* struck *Tirpitz*'s side at a depth of 20ft, and

A DAVID AND GOLIATH CONTEST: A MIDGET SUBMARINE VERSUS THE PRIDE OF THE GERMAN FLEET.

slid under the keel. They jettisoned the first 2-ton charge near the front of the ship, the second near the rear.

The charges were intended to detonate an hour after being set, but as the timers were not reliable Place knew he had to get as far away from the *Tirpitz* as fast as he could. But the *X-7* got tangled in the nets yet again, and was still stuck when the charges went off, blowing them clear of the net. The blast caused damage to the compasses and diving gauges. The submarine was now very difficult to control. Place desperately tried to manoeuvre the submarine but surfaced several times, each time coming under fire from the guns of the *Tirpitz*. This caused further damage to the hull and periscope.

With almost all their high-pressure air exhausted, Place sat *X-7* on the seabed while he considered his options. There was only enough air to get to the surface once more. He decided they would have to abandon ship.

When the *X-7* reached the surface, Place clambered out of the submarine and waved a white sweater. As he did so, the submarine capsized and sank. One officer escaped three hours later, but the other two men were drowned.

Place was taken prisoner, along with his surviving officer and the crew of *X-6*. The third submarine, *X-5*, sank with all hands. The prisoners were taken to Marlag-Milag Nord prison camp in Germany, where they spent the rest of the war. The *Tirpitz* was not sunk by the charges set by the two midget submarines, but she sustained serious damage that stopped her going to sea until April 1944.

Place and Cameron were still prisoners-of-war when they heard that they had been awarded Victoria Crosses for their supreme courage,

The *Tirpitz*, pride of the German fleet, at anchorage in the Norwegian fjords. The Germans had taken great efforts to protect their immense battleship, but they had not anticipated a bold attack by midget submarines. (IWM, HU 35755)

Sextant from the *X-7*, recovered from the bottom of the Kåfjord. (IWM, OPT 318)

endurance and utter contempt for danger. Place's actions were considered completely consistent with his character by his friends.

After the war Place resumed his naval career. In 1950 he made the unusual career choice of transferring to the Fleet Air Arm. He qualified as a pilot and served as a pilot and squadron commander in the Korean War. By 1968, Rear-Admiral Place was the only serving VC in the Royal Navy. After retirement from the Navy, he was chairman of the Victoria Cross and George Cross Association for 23 years until a few months before his death in 1994.

PERCY HOWARD HANSEN VC

9 August 1915

Portrait of Percy Hansen (1890–1951). Hansen was a 24-year-old officer when he saved six men from being burnt to death. (IWM, VC 527)

Percy Hansen is one of four Danes to have received the Victoria Cross. He was born in Germany to Danish parents, but he grew up in England and attended the Royal Military Academy, Sandhurst. In July 1915, Captain Hansen sailed for Gallipoli with the 6th Battalion, Lincolnshire Regiment. Fierce fighting had been raging between the Allies and the Turks on the narrow peninsula of Gallipoli since the ambitious Allied landings in April.

Hansen's battalion landed at Suvla Bay on 7 August, and successfully pushed up onto high ground. A few days later, they were ordered to try and take further high ground.

The battalion came under heavy small arms fire as soon as the attack was launched on 9 August. The Lincolns immediately started taking casualties, but struggled on up the slope until they finally took their objective. The fighting caused several small fires to break out as the battle continued. Most died down, but one set alight the dry scrub on the hillside, driving back the attackers. As the Lincolns retreated from the fire, there were too many wounded to carry away and around 20 wounded men remained on the burning hillside.

Realising the men could not escape, Percy Hansen called for volunteers to join him in his desperate mission. He set off over 300 yards of open ground, running through the burning scrub, dodging bullets and breathing in smoke, to try to rescue the men left on the hill. He made six trips, saving six men from being burnt alive.

For his bravery he was recommended for the Victoria Cross. Just weeks later, he showed his mettle again by swimming along the coast alone at night to find an enemy sniper and gun position that had been harassing the brigade's

position. But in September he fell ill with dysentery and was evacuated. While in hospital in Egypt, he learned he had been awarded the Victoria Cross for his actions on 9 August. Back in London undergoing further treatment, he was told he had also been awarded the Military Cross for his brave

Cigarette case given to Percy Hansen engraved with details of his VC. (IWM, EPH 9449, lent by Mr Charles Hansen Kessler)

solo reconnaissance mission. There was little good news in the autumn of 1915 and Hansen's exploits were widely covered in the press. He was hailed as a hero, and enjoyed being the toast of London society. He was finally fit for duty in February 1916 and spent the rest of the war on the Western Front. Hansen remained in the Army until after the Second World War, eventually retiring as a brigadier in 1946.

Percy Hansen's medal group. (Lent by Mr Charles Hansen Kessler)

John Bythesea (1827–1906). (Topfoto)

John Bythesea VC

9–12 August 1854

John Bythesea was born in Somerset in 1827. His four older brothers had all gone into the Army, but he broke with tradition and entered the Royal Navy in 1841. He was promoted to lieutenant in 1849, and joined HMS *Arrogant* in 1850. In 1854, the *Arrogant* joined Admiral Napier's fleet in the Baltic during the Crimean War.

Above left: Bythesea's miniature medal which he wore when not in uniform. (Courtesy of the Lord Ashcroft Collection) Above right: Bythesea and Johnstone overpower the couriers in this illustration. (© Illustrated London News/Mary Evans)

While on duty one day, Bythesea heard that mail from the tsar was being landed on the nearby island of Wårdö on the way to the Russian general at the fortress of Bomarsund. These secret dispatches contained information which would give the British a huge advantage if they could get their hands on them. As soon as he could, Bythesea searched the ship until he found a Swedish-speaking sailor, William Johnstone, who was prepared to accompany him on the dangerous mission and help him communicate with the locals. The ship's captain reluctantly gave permission for the pair to try and intercept the mail, thinking that just two men would never succeed in ambushing a larger group of the enemy in enemy territory.

Bythesea and Johnstone rowed to Wårdö on 9 August. With help from a local farmer, they hid for three days, at constant risk of discovery, disguised as local peasants. When the mail-bags were landed on 12 August, the pair laid in wait until the military escort had departed. Bythesea, armed with his pistol, leapt out from the bushes, closely followed by Johnstone. Two of the five couriers immediately dropped their bags and ran. The other three surrendered as they assumed Bythesea and Johnstone were part of a much larger force. Bythesea took the three men prisoner, marched them back to their own boat, and forced the Russian captives to row them back to the *Arrogant*.

The mail was sent on to Admiral Napier, and Bomarsund was taken just four days later using the information in the mail. This audacious ambush required true boldness against such superior numbers. Both men were awarded the newly established Victoria Cross, and Bythesea was the second man to be decorated by Queen Victoria at the first investiture of the decoration in Hyde Park in 1857.

Bythesea continued his career on various naval vessels for nearly two decades. Unfortunately in 1872 the *Lord Clyde* ran aground while under his command trying to help a stranded steamer. For allowing his ship to run aground, Bythesea was court-martialled, dismissed from his ship and banned from being employed at sea. But his naval career was not over as two years later, he was appointed Consulting Naval Officer to the Indian government, overseeing the remodelling of the Indian Navy. He finally retired in 1877 as a rear-admiral.

THE SECOND-EVER VICTORIA CROSS ACTION.

DAPHNE PEARSON GC

31 May 1940

Daphne Pearson (1911–2000) painted in 1940 by Dame Laura Knight. Pearson was a photographer with her own studio before the Second World War. After the war she trained in horticulture. (IWM, ART LD 626)

Joan Daphne Pearson was an adventurous woman who ran her own photography business and learnt to fly in the 1930s. She was only a few hours away from gaining her pilot's certificate when the Second World War broke out. She joined the Auxiliary Territorial Service in 1939, and transferred to the Women's Auxiliary Air Force establishment attached to No. 500 Squadron, based at RAF Detling. Corporal Pearson worked in the sick bay at Detling, where she was kept busy attending to wounded airmen.

In the early hours of 31 May she was woken by the sound of an aircraft in distress. Looking out of the window she saw a bomber approaching with one engine on fire; a crash seemed inevitable. She dressed and rushed out just in time to see the aircraft crash on the outskirts of the airfield. One bomb exploded as the aircraft crashed, instantly killing the wireless operator and injuring the rest of the crew. A guard tried to stop her, but she pushed past, scrambling through undergrowth until she reached the burning wreckage. She climbed onto the aircraft, released the pilot's parachute harness and dragged him away.

Pearson stopped to administer first aid as he was groaning in pain. She could see he had a neck injury but when he mumbled that the aircraft was fully loaded with bombs, she knew they had to get further away. She carefully moved him, reaching the other side of a ridge as the petrol tanks exploded. She protected him with her body, placing her helmet on his head. She kept his head still to prevent further dislocation, and administered first aid as the bombs continued to explode.

Finally the pilot was taken away by ambulance. Explosions continued, but Pearson still insisted on going back to the wreckage to look for the missing fourth crew-member. She then returned to base to help the doctor and was on duty at 8am that morning as usual.

She was awarded the Empire Gallantry Medal on 19 July 1940 for her courageous and prompt actions which had undoubtedly saved the pilot's life. She was the first woman to receive a gallantry award during the Second World War. When the Empire Gallantry Medal was revoked and replaced by the George Cross Pearson was presented with a George Cross by George VI in 1941.

Pearson was commissioned in 1940 and served most of the rest of the war with Bomber Command, despite suffering bouts of ill-health. She enjoyed a varied post-war career including work in the prison service and at the Royal Botanical Gardens, Kew, before emigrating to Australia.

Section of a letter written by Pearson to her mother, describing the crash on 31 May 1940. (IWM Department of Documents JDM 24424)

FIRST WOMAN TO RECEIVE THE GEORGE CROSS.

DUNCAN BOYES VC

6 September 1864

Duncan Gordon Boyes was born in 1846 in Cheltenham, the youngest of five brothers. He joined his first ship, the HMS *Virago*, at the age of 13. Four years later, Midshipman Boyes was serving in HMS *Euryalus* off Japan. The *Euryalus* was the flagship of a multi-national squadron trying to force the opening of the Straits of Shimonoseki, which had been closed by the renegade Imperial Prince Hagato.

On 6 September, the naval forces landed and destroyed two Japanese batteries. As they prepared to return to their ships, part of the brigade were suddenly attacked by a strong body of Japanese. The Japanese troops were driven back and the British then discovered a large fort, well defended by guns, at the head of the valley. They had to take the fort before night fell and left them stranded in enemy territory.

The Colours carried by Boyes at Shimonoseki. The six bullet-holes are clearly visible. (© National Maritime Museum, Greenwich, London)

Duncan Boyes (1846–69). Boyes featured in a series of posters, 'Victoria Crosses on the Victoria Line' in 2004. The series was the idea of Boyes' great-nephew. (IWM, VC 113)

Under heavy fire, the British Naval Brigade advanced up one side of the valley, and the Royal Marines advanced up the other. Boyes carried the Colours for the naval brigade, providing a rallying point and focus at the front of the attack. Boyes was a clear target for the Japanese defenders but he did not hesitate for a moment, even when one colour sergeant was killed. Eventually Boyes was ordered to stop. Boyes and the surviving colour sergeant were both badly wounded. The Colours had been pierced by six bullets. But he still hesitated, determined to finish the job. Eventually Boyes, severely wounded, was evacuated from the battlefield.

Boyes was awarded the Victoria Cross. Along with the other two recipients from the action, Boyes was presented with his medal at an elaborate ceremony when the ship returned to England. It was to be the high point of Boyes' life.

Tragically, just a few years later, he was court-martialled for breaking into the Naval Yard at Bermuda after 11pm. He admitted guilt, and was dismissed from the service. Boyes was apparently depressed following the disgrace of his dismissal, perhaps feeling he had failed to uphold the honour of the Victoria Cross. If so, it cannot have helped that his sister was married to Thomas Young, an Indian Mutiny VC.

He moved to New Zealand, living on his brother's sheep station in Otago Province. He was drinking heavily, and then suffered a nervous breakdown. He killed himself in 1869, aged just 22.

His Victoria Cross was bought by his old school, Cheltenham College, in 1978, and then sold in 1998, the money from the sale being used to set up a scholarship in Boyes' name.

Ian Edward Fraser VC
James Joseph Magennis VC

31 July 1945

After the *Tirpitz* raid, several X-craft were adapted for use in the Far East. In 1945, two of these new XE-class submarines were deployed to sink two 10,000-ton Japanese cruisers, the *Takao* and *Mikyo*, anchored off Singapore. Though damaged and unable to set sail, these ships still posed a serious threat as floating gun-batteries. The submarine tasked to mine the *Takao* was the *XE-3*, under the command of Lieutenant Ian Fraser, and crewed by the No.1, Sub-Lieutenant William Smith, helmsman, Engine Room Artificer Charles Reid, and the diver, Leading Seaman James Magennis.

Fraser and Magennis both went to sea as teenagers. Fraser joined the Merchant Navy in the mid-1930s then joined the Royal Navy on the outbreak of the Second World War. Belfast-born Magennis joined the Royal Navy in 1935. Both men spent the first few years of the war on destroyers before volunteering for the submarine service, then for 'special and hazardous service': midget submarines. Magennis had already served as passage crew for *X-7* for the *Tirpitz* raid in 1943, when he was mentioned in dispatches.

The first challenge for the two midget submarines was to travel 35 miles from their towing submarine to the Johore Straits without being detected. Fraser chose to navigate the minefields rather than risk coming within range of the Japanese listening post.

The actual suit worn by Magennis during the raid on the *Takao*. Two of Magennis' comrades had died a few weeks before the *Takao* attack in diving accidents, probably from oxygen poisoning, which makes his determination to get the job done even more remarkable. (IWM, EQU 2204)

James Magennis VC (1919–86) and Ian Fraser VC (1920–2008). (IWM, A 26940A)

Approaching at night, he was lucky enough to find the defence boom open. He made his way up the straits, and rested near to where they thought the ship was moored. When daylight came they found that they were in fact sitting in a Japanese minefield.

Finally they reached the *Takao*, around ten miles up the channel from the boom. The raid nearly ended in disaster when Fraser hit the *Takao*'s hull on his first attack. But they remained undetected, and on the second attempt they successfully slid under the ship. Fraser now found that the water was so shallow that the cruiser was almost resting on the bottom. Under the middle section was a 24ft hole, so after much manoeuvring, Fraser squeezed the *XE-3* between cruiser and sea-bed so the mines could be attached to the hull. Because of the shape of the *Takao*'s hull, the hatch could only be opened halfway and Magennis had to squeeze out through the tiny gap, damaging his diving equipment.

Before Magennis could attach the limpet mines, he had to scrape barnacles and seaweed off the hull with his knife. But it became clear that they would not attach and he was forced to return to the submarine to get rope so that the mines could be tied on. Magennis persisted until he had

Mini-submarines were cramped, even for shorter men like Fraser, who was 5ft 4in. (IWM, A 30568, Courtesy of the Lord Ashcroft Collection)

Fraser and Magennis in action, as depicted in *The Victor* in 1961. (*The Victor* © D. C. Thomson & Co., Ltd)

attached all six, each of which weighed 200lb. It took him around half an hour. All the time, oxygen bubbles were rising to the surface from a leak in his suit. The water was very clear, and the chances of being seen were high. When he finally squeezed back into the submarine, Magennis was utterly exhausted, and his hands were cut to pieces by the barnacles.

The *XE-3* had to escape before the mines exploded, but the tide had gone out, and they found themselves stuck under the *Takao*. Fraser finally managed to get free after 20 minutes of struggling. But when he tried to jettison the explosive side charges the submarine was carrying, one would not release. The mini-submarine was lying in just 15ft of clear water, only 50ft from the *Takao*. Despite his total exhaustion, Magennis went out again. It took him seven minutes with a heavy spanner to release the second charge.

Fraser finally guided the *XE-3* safely out of the channel, and they were 15 miles away when the mines blew a large hole in the *Takao*. The crew of the *XE-3* had been on alert, at their stations, for over 50 hours in cramped

and difficult conditions. All four were decorated, with Fraser and Magennis both being awarded the Victoria Cross.

After the war, Fraser and some other ex-frogmen set up a show where divers re-enacted wartime exploits in a 20,000-gallon glass-sided tank. Fraser was criticised by some for trading on his Victoria Cross, but the show was very popular, enabling him to start his own diving company. In 1957 he published his autobiography, *Frogman VC*, recounting his wartime exploits and his post-war business experiences. Fraser remained on the Royal Navy Reserve list until the mid-1960s.

Magennis left the Navy in 1949 and returned to Belfast with his family. The people of Belfast had given Magennis a gift of over £3,000 when he was awarded his VC. But by 1952, Magennis had spent it all, so after losing his job he sold his VC. When the story was reported in the newspapers, it was used against him by those on both sides of the sectarian divide. Eventually, he left Belfast with his family and spent the rest of his life in Yorkshire, working as an electrician. A memorial to Magennis now stands in front of Belfast City Hall.

MAGENNIS WAS THE ONLY SECOND WORLD WAR VICTORIA CROSS RECIPIENT FROM NORTHERN IRELAND.

GEOFFREY CHARLES TASKER KEYES VC

18 November 1941

Geoffrey Keyes (1917–41). He left a letter for his family to open in the case of his death stating: 'This is a wonderful opportunity which, if it succeeds, will help the cause. Don't worry about me.' (Topfoto, PA)

Geoffrey Keyes originally wanted to follow his father, Admiral of the Fleet Sir Roger Keyes, into the Royal Navy. Foiled by his poor eyesight, instead he joined his uncle's regiment, the Royal Scots Greys, as a second lieutenant. After the outbreak of war he volunteered for special service and then joined the newly created Commando organisation.

By 1941, Keyes was the youngest lieutenant-colonel in the Army, in command of No.11 Scottish Commando, and he had already been awarded the Military Cross for bravery. He was just 24. That autumn, Keyes was involved in planning raids on targets behind enemy lines in North Africa. Keyes selected for himself the most hazardous target, the assassination of Field Marshal Erwin Rommel, commander of the German forces in North Africa. It was thought that Rommel was based at a villa at Sidi Rafa, Libya, 250 miles behind German lines. Even success would almost certainly end in the raiders' deaths, but Keyes would not be deterred.

On 13 November, Keyes and his men landed on a beach from a submarine far behind enemy lines. The chances of success were immediately reduced when half his force could not land due to deteriorating weather conditions. The following evening those men who had successfully landed set out in the pouring rain, travelling over extremely difficult terrain in the dead of night. It took them several days to reach their target, and they finally crept close on 17 November. More rain hampered their final approach to the villa, which was up a steep slope.

At the summit, the party split. Keyes took two men, Captain Campbell and Sergeant Terry, with him to attack the main villa. They crawled into the garden, past the armed guards, and up to the house. Running up the steps to the front door, they beat upon the door, demanding entrance in German. Overpowering the sentry, they burst into the house. Keyes began to check the rooms. The second room had around ten men in it. Keyes opened the door and fired into the room several times. As he re-opened the door for Campbell to throw in a grenade, he was shot above the heart. The others carried him out, but by the time they laid him down on the ground outside he was already dead.

All but two of the raiders were killed or captured. Rommel was actually in Rome at the time, and it is disputed whether he ever used the villa at all. However, when he heard of the raid, Rommel ordered his chaplain to bury Keyes with full military honours. The chaplain later wrote to Keyes' parents telling them how much the Germans had admired his courage. Keyes' raid was one of the most daring actions of the Second World War, and his actions are all the more astounding because he knew that he was very unlikely to return. His Victoria Cross was awarded to his grieving parents at a private audience with the king at Buckingham Palace.

Keyes shown shooting the sentry on duty, although it was actually German-speaking Campbell who did this. (National Archives)

ISRAEL HARDING VC

11 July 1882

Israel Harding (1833–1917). (IWM, LI 2009 999 66 2, Courtesy of the Lord Ashcroft Collection)

Born in Portsmouth into a large family with a distinguished naval heritage, Israel Harding joined the Royal Navy as a cabin boy while in his teens. After training in gunnery, he served in Royal Navy ships around the world for the next 40 years. While Gunner of HMS *Gladiator* in 1871, he helped put out a fire at a munitions factory in Brazil, for which he was awarded a Brazilian Medal.

In 1882, Harding was 48 years old, and the Gunner on HMS *Alexandra*. The *Alexandra*, flagship of Admiral Sir Beauchamp Seymour, was one of eight Royal Navy ships that bombarded Alexandria, Egypt, for ten hours on 11 July 1882, while under heavy fire from rioters onshore.

During the bombardment, a 10in shell pierced the ship's side and landed on the main deck, not far from a magazine which contained 25 tons of gunpowder. Hearing the shouts, Harding rushed up the ladder from below. Taking in the situation at a glance, he threw some water from a nearby bucket over the shell, then picked up the shell and submerged it in the bucket, extinguishing it. His actions probably saved the lives of many of his comrades.

Harding carrying the shell to the tub of water. (IWM, LI 2009 999 66 2, Courtesy of the Lord Ashcroft Collection)

He was mentioned in dispatches by the Commander-in-Chief for his bravery and quick-thinking, promoted to Chief Gunner, and later awarded the Victoria Cross. The shell was kept, and presented to the Prince of Wales as a momento of the bombardment of Alexandria.

On retirement from the Royal Navy, Harding settled down in his hometown of Portsmouth. He married twice and had a son and six daughters. Remarkably his naval career was not at an end. During the First World War, he served on minesweepers, even though he was in his eighties. For this he was promoted to lieutenant on the retired list. He died in 1917, bequeathing his medals individually to his children in his will. A new accommodation block at HMS *Excellent* on Whale Island, Portsmouth, was named after Harding in 2009.

> '*My own course of action was decided upon as quick as thought. I just picked up that shell, and flung it into a tub full of water.*'
> **Israel Harding, *The Strand* magazine, 1896**

Those medals awarded to Israel Harding now in Lord Ashcroft's collection. (Courtesy of the Lord Ashcroft Collection)

HAROLD REGINALD NEWGASS GC

3 December 1940

Harold Newgass (1896–1984). He was in the Territorial Army from 1918 until 1934, when he left with the rank of captain. He served in the RNVR for most of the Second World War. (IWM, Newgass 001, by permission of The Hon. Mrs P.C. Baillie)

In September 1940, the Luftwaffe began a systematic bombing campaign against British cities, it became known as the Blitz. The same month, 41-year-old Harold Newgass joined the Royal Naval Volunteer Reserve. He had previously volunteered for service with the Territorial Army during the First World War, but the Armistice was declared before he reached the front in 1918.

While Newgass was undergoing RNVR training, a call went out for volunteers to carry out special duties. He was one of the volunteers selected to undergo a rapid but intensive course in bomb disposal work. Just days after finishing his training he was defusing unexploded bombs. Two months later he was already an expert, much in demand as the Luftwaffe carried out widespread attacks using large bombs dropped on small parachutes which became known as parachute mines.

At the end of November, Liverpool was heavily bombed, and Lieutenant Newgass was in charge of a naval party sent there to clear unexploded mines. One of them, a German magnetic mine, had fallen through the crown of a gasholder holding 2,000,000 cubic feet of gas at Garston gasworks. The port of Garston was paralysed. Six thousand people were evacuated, and the gas supply to half of Liverpool was endangered.

Due to the difficult and crucial nature of this disposal, Newgass decided to do it on his own.

The mine rested on the floor of the gasholder, nose-down in 7ft of oily water. It took 30 hours to pump out the water, leaving the mine in several inches of sludgy coal tar in the bottom of the pitch-black gasholder surrounded by a highly flammable, noxious atmosphere.

On 3 December, Newgass finally prepared to enter the gasholder. He needed to use breathing equipment because of the toxic atmosphere inside. Six oxygen cylinders were available, each of them lasting just 30 minutes.

Newgass had to enter the gasholder through a hole in the crown, and his first task was to take all his tools down a ladder into the gasholder, and inspect the situation. He was well aware that once inside the gasholder there was no chance of escape if the clock on the mine started to tick.

Harold Newgass' medal group. (IWM, OMD 2900–2906)

Newgass (on left) and others sitting on a defused mine in Milford Haven. The work of the bomb disposal teams throughout Britain during the Second World War was both physically and mentally draining. Newgass performed this work for five long years and his actions in Liverpool in December 1940 were just one example of his remarkable service. (IWM, HU 58436, by permission of The Hon. Mrs P.C. Baillie)

The electro-mechanical fuse timer that Newgass removed from the mine in the gasholder. (IWM, MUN 3867 A)

On his third trip into the gasholder he placed sandbags around the mine, and lashed it to a roof support. On his fourth trip he carefully turned the mine, removing the fuse, primer and detonator. Fighting exhaustion from the hard physical effort as well as the difficulty of breathing through the unfamiliar apparatus he made a fifth trip down into the gasholder. This time he turned the mine again and delicately undid the clock keep ring. Finally on his last trip he withdrew the clock, making the mine safe. It had taken him three hours of gruelling work, and considerable physical effort to defuse the mine. His work that day was recognised among his peers as probably the most difficult and dangerous assignment that mine-disposal men had ever handled. Today it is still acknowledged as one of the most skilful detonations under extremely difficult circumstances ever performed.

For his efforts, he was recommended for the new George Cross. As a gesture of appreciation he received a gold cigarette case from the gasworks, and the employees clubbed together to buy him a pair of gold cuff-links. He also received presents from the people whose homes he had protected.

He carried on in similar work for another four years, saving many lives, until deemed medically unfit to carry on. He attained the rank of lieutenant-commander. Harold Newgass died in 1984.

John Edmund Commerell VC
William Thomas Rickard VC

11 October 1855

Edmund Commerell (1829–1901). Edmund Rock and Commerell Point in British Columbia are both named after him. (IWM, VC 01, Courtesy of the Lord Ashcroft Collection)

John Edmund Commerell was already an experienced naval officer when he took command of HMS *Weser* at the age of 26 in 1855 during the Crimean War. He had joined the Navy as a teenager and had served in China and South America. The *Weser* was cruising along the eastern side of the Spit of Arabat in the Sea of Azov when Commerell learned that Russian stores of 400 tons of corn and forage, intended for the use of the garrison at Sebastopol, were stockpiled nearby. To destroy the supplies would require a difficult and dangerous journey deep behind Russian lines, nonetheless Commerell organised and undertook this daring raid, accompanied by two volunteers: Quartermaster William Rickard and Seaman George Milestone. Rickard, like his commanding officer, was highly experienced, having spent years in both the Royal Navy and Merchant Navy. He had fought in the Naval Brigade at the Alma and Inkerman during earlier periods of the Crimea.

Under cover of darkness, the raiding party, accompanied by two other volunteers, left the *Weser* in a small boat, and rowed to the Spit of Arabat.

This narrow strip of land separates the Sea of Azov from a salt-water lagoon known as the Putrid Sea (today referred to as the Sivash Lake). After dragging the boat across the sandy spit in darkness, which was reportedly 'swarming' with Russians, they then rowed across the Putrid Sea before reaching the Crimean shore. Two volunteer seamen stayed with the boat, while the other three set off across land on foot. They had to cover two and a half miles undetected, wading across two rivers.

Finally, they reached the Russian store, on the far

William Thomas Rickard (1828–1905). (IWM, VC 1051)

bank of the second river. Approaching with caution, they set the stacks ablaze. The flames brought Russian troops running, and the raiders were pursued back to the shore by both Cossack cavalry and infantry, under heavy musket fire. The cavalry could not follow them into the muddy ground by the shore. However Milestone was now so exhausted that he fell into the mud and could not drag himself out. He begged to be left behind, but Rickard went back to drag him free, even though the Russians were firing

John Commerell's medal group. For the action Rickard was also awarded a medal for distinguished conduct, and the Légion d'Honneur. (Courtesy of the Lord Ashcroft Collection)

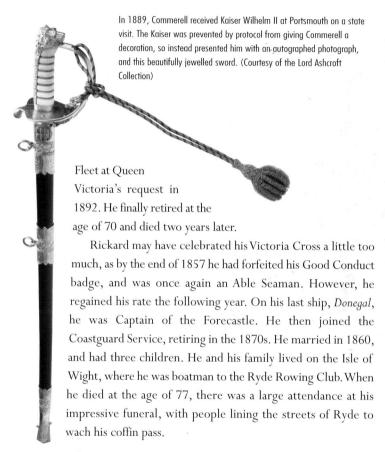

In 1889, Commerell received Kaiser Wilhelm II at Portsmouth on a state visit. The Kaiser was prevented by protocol from giving Commerell a decoration, so instead presented him with an autographed photograph, and this beautifully jewelled sword. (Courtesy of the Lord Ashcroft Collection)

at them from only 40 yards away. Rickard and Commerell removed Milestone's boots and half-carried him to the boat. They then completed the return journey across the lagoon, dragged their boat back across the spit, again under fire, and made their way out to the ship. Look-outs later confirmed that the stacks had burnt to the ground, denying the Russians crucial supplies.

Commerell and Rickard were awarded the Victoria Cross for the daring raid, Rickard receiving his on the personal recommendation of Commerell. Commerell saw action around the world before a lung wound forced him to resign his command in 1873. Over the next 25 years Commerell continued to collect honours and promotions. He was a Conservative MP for several years, campaigning for the strengthening of the Navy. He was made Admiral of the Fleet at Queen Victoria's request in 1892. He finally retired at the age of 70 and died two years later.

Rickard may have celebrated his Victoria Cross a little too much, as by the end of 1857 he had forfeited his Good Conduct badge, and was once again an Able Seaman. However, he regained his rate the following year. On his last ship, *Donegal*, he was Captain of the Forecastle. He then joined the Coastguard Service, retiring in the 1870s. He married in 1860, and had three children. He and his family lived on the Isle of Wight, where he was boatman to the Ryde Rowing Club. When he died at the age of 77, there was a large attendance at his impressive funeral, with people lining the streets of Ryde to watch his coffin pass.

Job Henry Charles Drain VC
Frederick Luke VC

26 August 1914

The opening days of the First World War saw the British forced to retreat from Mons in Belgium. On 26 August, the British Expeditionary Force's II Corps fought the second major battle of the war, at Le Cateau. It was bloody and relentless, with the Allies tenaciously holding their ground for several hours. Eventually forced to retreat in the face of overwhelming numbers, the order was given to withdraw the all-important guns. One of the batteries present was the 37th (Howitzer) Battery, Royal Field Artillery. The battery had already taken heavy casualties, and there were simply not enough teams to move all the guns. With the Germans now only 100 yards away, two guns still remained. The captain of the battery, Douglas Reynolds, collected volunteers for what was surely a suicidal mission to try and save the guns. There was no shortage of willing men and two of the volunteers who stepped forward were Driver Job Drain and Driver Frederick Luke, both aged just 18.

The horses of two gun teams galloped forward. Both guns were successfully limbered to their horse teams. Drain was the lead driver, and Luke the wheel driver, of the first howitzer. The Germans now brought heavy fire to bear on them. The team's centre driver, Cobey, was shot from his horse. The team of the other gun was shot before they could get their gun away. Drain, Luke and Reynolds urged their horses on under intense fire, finally reaching safety and successfully saving their gun. Drain said of it 'it was a ride of either life or death.' They were the only three to return of the dozen men who had gone out to get the guns.

Drain, Luke and Reynolds were awarded the Victoria Cross for their bravery and presented with their medals on the battlefield by George V. Luke later remembered that the king had told him not to drop his medal in the mud! Le Cateau became a battle honour latter used by 93rd (Le Cateau) Field Battery, and troops were named after the men as a testament to their brave actions in the face of overwhelming odds.

Job Drain (1895–1975). A statue commemorating him was unveiled in Barking in 2009. (IWM, VC 349)

Frederick Luke (1895–1983). After the war, Luke settled in Glasgow with his wife. He became an engineer, and was a school janitor for many years. (IWM, Q 67942)

This depiction of the action at Le Cateau was painted by a friend of Reynolds. Luke had a print of it on his wall in later life. (Mary Evans)

Captain Reynolds died of wounds in France in 1916. Luke, a native of Hampshire who had joined the Royal Horse Artillery in 1913, was wounded at Ypres, but returned to the front to fight at the Somme and Cambrai. He stayed in the Army until 1922, when he left with the rank of sergeant. When the Second World War broke out, he joined the RAF Regiment.

Drain went through the First World War without a scratch, becoming a sergeant. He then returned home to Barking, where he was feted as Barking's first VC. He hardly ever spoke about his medal, and found it difficult to adjust to civilian life and find work, eventually becoming a London bus driver and later working for London Electricity Board.

George Leslie Drewry VC
Wilfred St Aubyn Malleson VC
George McKenzie Samson VC
Edward Unwin VC
William Charles Williams VC

25 April 1915

On 25 April 1915, the Allies landed on the Gallipoli peninsula. The Turks were ready and waiting, and the men wading ashore received a murderous welcome.

Alongside the open boats that landed at V Beach, a converted collier, the SS *River Clyde*, was run aground. The idea was for the 2,000 men inside to land quickly on the beach and reinforce those who had just landed from the nearby boats. It was, as many soldiers said, a modern Trojan horse. A long flat-bottomed boat known as a hopper was intended to bridge the gap between the collier and the beach, providing a platform for the soldiers to charge quickly across. This plan had been formulated by Commander Edward Unwin, a retired naval officer, who had rejoined the Navy the previous year from the reserve.

At around 6.30am on 25 April, Unwin steered the *River Clyde* in. He had a difficult approach, but to begin with all was quiet. Then, as the open boats grounded, a devastating fire burst out across the beach. Many men from the boats were killed or wounded before they reached the shore, as the troops inside the *River Clyde* realised with horror what was happening. But the plan to connect the *Clyde* to the beach also now went horribly wrong. The collier grounded further out from the beach than planned, and the hopper swung off to the side. Midshipman George Drewry and Leading Seaman George

George Leslie Drewry (1894–1918). Drewry was only 20, but had already seen much of the world since joining the Merchant Navy, and had even been shipwrecked on a desert island. He had joined the Royal Naval Reserve in 1913, and was called up on the outbreak of war. Drewry attained the rank of lieutenant, before being killed in an accident at sea at Scapa Flow in 1918. (IWM, Q 79788)

Samson unsuccessfully tried to link the hopper to the *River Clyde*, but it was impossible.

As soon as he saw what was happening, 51-year-old Unwin, accompanied by Able Seaman William Williams, immediately left the safety of the ship to try to make a new bridge for the soldiers. The pair waded to the beach and pulled round some small boats that had been towed alongside the *River Clyde* just in case they were needed. Once the boats were in place,

WILLIAMS WAS THE FIRST-EVER POSTHUMOUS NAVAL VICTORIA CROSS.

Unwin and Williams stood waist-deep in the cold water, holding fast to the lighters for over an hour, until Williams was killed by a shell. Soon after, Unwin collapsed from exhaustion, and was taken back to the *River Clyde*. Drewry now used longer rope to tie the boats to some rocks, and the men started to pour over the bridge once again.

But the boats came loose again, and Drewry swam between the lighters, trying to run lines between them. He suffered a head wound, but he bound it up, and tried to swim a rope across again before having to eventually retire,

George McKenzie Samson (1889–1923). Seaman Samson had had an adventurous life as a merchant seaman, and as a driver on the Turkish railway, before being called up from the reserve for duty in the First World War. He was hit in 19 places at Gallipoli but after recovering made several unsuccessful attempts to return to active service. After the war he rejoined the Merchant Navy, and died of pneumonia at sea. He was buried in Bermuda with full honours. (IWM, VC 1103)

Wilfred St Aubyn Malleson (centre) (1896–1975). In a naval career lasting until 1947, Malleson later attained the rank of captain. (IWM, HU 35958)

Unwin and Williams found there was nothing to tie them to on the shore. So they tied the ropes to themselves and the soldiers started to cross. The Turkish defenders started to concentrate on the bridge of boats, which was soon piled with bodies and the water ran red with blood. When he saw what Unwin was desperately trying to do, Drewry crossed through the water to help him.

Painting of the *River Clyde* at Gallipoli by Charles Dixon. The adaptations that Unwin ordered — doors cut into the ship's sides and gangways — can be seen. It is worth noting that the uniforms are wrong. (Bridgeman)

Edward Unwin (1864–1950). At the evacuation of Gallipoli, Unwin was principal beachmaster at Suvla, and was given the honour of being the last to leave. In January 1917 he became Principal Naval Transport Officer in the Eastern Mediterranean. He finally retired in 1920, and was granted the rank of Captain. (IWM, Q 85893)

exhausted by his efforts. Midshipman Wilfred Malleson now took over his work, and when the securing line was shot through, Malleson made two attempts to re-secure it, all under heavy fire. After a short rest, Unwin rejoined his crew and fixed lines again, but was wounded in the face, then again overcome by exhaustion. Eventually the landing was halted as casualties continued to rise, but was later completed under cover of darkness, when the rest of the soldiers filed off the shot-riddled ship, without sustaining a casualty.

The rest of the day was spent trying to help wounded soldiers. Later in the day, Unwin went out once more, taking a lifeboat to save wounded men

DREWRY WAS THE FIRST OFFICER OF RNR AND MERCHANT SERVICE TO RECEIVE THE VICTORIA CROSS.

Able Seaman William Williams (1880–1915). He had served 15 years with the Navy, and had been recalled to active duty in 1914. He had begged Unwin to allow him to come on the *River Clyde* to V Beach. Unwin ordered him to stay with him, which he did until he was killed.

An incredible picture taken by a machine gunner in the bows of the *River Clyde* during the landings on 25 April 1915. (IWM, Q50473)

lying in shallow water, until forced to stop from sheer exhaustion. After resting Drewry organised men to move the wounded from the hopper and lighters to a trawler. Samson worked on the hopper and boats all day, getting out lines to his crewmates, and helping the wounded from the beach to the hopper. He continued his work the next day until he was seriously wounded by machine gun fire.

For their extraordinary and sustained attempts to make the landings possible under heavy fire and impossible conditions, Unwin, Williams, Samson, Drewry and Malleson were all mentioned by name in a dispatch by Vice-Admiral de Robeck, who placed them at the head of a list of 'special recommendations'. On the basis of this, they were all awarded the Victoria Cross.

'Men were falling down like ninepins quite near us, and perhaps it was only the thought that we must give them a helping hand that made us forget our own danger.'
George McKenzie Samson

'Unwin has earned the VC several times over. He, with two midshipmen and two seamen, performed perfect prodigies of valour and heroism.'
Admiral Wemyss

PETER SCAWEN WATKINSON ROBERTS VC

16 February 1942

Peter Roberts entered the Royal Navy in 1935, and joined the submarine service in 1939. After serving in HMS *Tribune* as torpedo and gunnery officer, he became First Lieutenant in HMS *Thrasher*.

On 16 February 1942, HMS *Thrasher* was attacked by enemy aircraft and heavily depth-charged off Crete for over three hours. That night, when the submarine surfaced, unusual banging noises were heard. Two unexploded bombs were found on the submarine's casing, just forward of the 4in gun mounting. Roberts and Petty Officer Tommy Gould volunteered to remove the bombs.

HMS *Thrasher* after Roberts and Gould's VC action. 'B' marks where the first bomb was found on the casing. 'A' marks where the bomb penetrated the gun platform. 'A1' where the unexploded bomb was found inside the casing. Gould is standing in the casing hatch where he and Roberts entered the casing, and back to which they had to drag the bomb. (IWM, A 8710)

Peter Roberts (1917–79). He was a special-entry cadet into the Royal Navy from King's School, Canterbury. Roberts received his medal at Buckingham Palace on 4 July 1942. On his way home from his investiture he learned he had been awarded the DSC for gallantry on submarine patrols. He retired from the Navy in 1962 with the rank of lieutenant commander. (IWM, HU 1863)

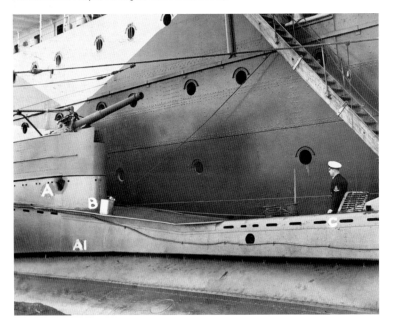

They wrapped the first bomb in an old potato sack, then carefully moved it to the bows and dropped it overboard, *Trasher* going full astern as they dropped it to get clear.

They then found the second bomb had pierced the casing, and was wedged between the casing and hull. To recover the 100lb bomb they had to wriggle through the confined space between the casing and the hull, around structures, battery ventilators, pipes and wires. In places the hull was only two feet from the casing. To get the bomb out through the casing, Gould lay on his back with the bomb cradled on his stomach. Roberts then lay on his

Roberts' action was depicted in *The Victor* in 1961. It shows Roberts and Gould pushing and pulling the bomb, instead of Roberts pulling Gould and the bomb. (*The Victor* © D. C. Thomson & Co., Ltd)

stomach, pulling Gould by his shoulders while moving cautiously backwards through the pitch-black, wet casing. The bomb was making worrying noises, and the submarine was being continually buffeted by the waves. There was a large chance of attack as they were so close to the enemy coast. Roberts and Gould knew that if the submarine was attacked, the captain would be forced to crash-dive, drowning both men. It took Roberts 40 minutes to drag Gould and the bomb 20 feet back to the grating. They were then able to pass the bomb up, wrap it and then lower it carefully over the side.

They had saved their crewmates, and the submarine, enabling *Thrasher* to continue her operational patrol. The captain noted the incident in the patrol report, and commended Roberts and Gould for their excellent conduct. Several months later it was announced that Roberts and Gould had been awarded the Victoria Cross. The Honours and Awards Committee had in fact initially opposed the recommendation, as their bravery had not been in the presence of the enemy. The Commander-in-Chief Mediterranean, Admiral Sir Andrew Cunningham persuaded them that two enemy bombs, in a submarine near the enemy coast, was quite enough enemy presence to warrant the Victoria Cross.

JAMES DUNDAS VC

30 April 1865

James Dundas (1842–79). (IWM, LO 2009 999 43 2, Courtesy of the Lord Ashcroft Collection)

Born in Edinburgh in 1842, James Dundas trained at Addiscombe College. He was appointed lieutenant in the Bengal Engineers, Indian Army, at the age of 18 and sailed for India. In 1865, Dundas' regiment took part in the Bhutan campaign. The British had sent a peace mission to Bhutan in 1864 after a recent civil war, but when the new government rejected Britain's treaty, the British advanced into Bhutan. At first they met only limited resistance by locals armed with primitive weaponry.

However, towards the end of the campaign, a large local force made a fierce attack on a British garrison at Dewan-Giri, causing it to be abandoned. On 30 April 1865, the British tried to recapture the position. After three hours of fighting under a hot sun they had successfully carried most of the position, but about 150–200 enemy barricaded themselves in the blockhouse. It was imperative that the blockhouse be taken as quickly as possibly before the rest of the force rallied. However, the men were tired, and reluctant to take on the position. Dundas and Captain William Trevor were ordered to lead the way.

The wall protecting the blockhouse was over 4 metres high. As the two men reached the top both were attacked. Dundas was hit on the head by a stone, knocking him to the bottom again. Trevor held off his first attacker, but then he too was hit on the head with a stone. But before he could be bludgeoned a second time, Dundas got back to the top of the wall and shot Trevor's attacker in the head.

Because the roof of the blockhouse was so close to the wall, Dundas and Trevor had to lower themselves head-first through the gap, and were immediately attacked from all sides.

As Dundas and Trevor dropped into the compound and disappeared from view, the Sikh soldiers, who had up until this point not responded to verbal commands, rushed to follow them. The fighting in the confined space was fierce and desperate. The British killed around 150 and wounded many, but only suffered six killed and 50 wounded.

James Dundas' medal group. (Courtesy of the Lord Ashcroft Collection)

Dundas and Trevor were amongst those wounded in the action. On the recommendation of the officer in command, both men were awarded the Victoria Cross for their boldness and gallantry in the attack. Dundas received his in Calcutta, India, several years after the action.

After the expedition, Dundas remained in India and joined the Public Works Department. In 1878 he saved a man from a burning house in Simla and in 1879, he chose to risk his life yet again by volunteering to serve in the Second Anglo-Afghan War. At Sherpur, a few days before Christmas, the Engineers were destroying several forts. Dundas and a lieutenant had constructed three mines at one fort. They withdrew their men to safety, and then proceeded to light the three fuses. Two of the mines were defective and exploded immediately, burying both men in the ruins of the fort. Dundas' body was recovered, and he was given a soldier's funeral. In 2002, the Royal Engineers named a rebuilt bridge near Kabul after this heroic man.

'Just as I was going to get it again Dundas reappeared on the field and blew out my stoner's brains.'
Captain William Trevor in a letter to his brother

AGGRESSION

'almost without halting in his rush ... shot and killed at least six'

For many actions killing is the means to the end. To prevail, maximum force has to be applied. As a quality, Aggression is hard and sharp, like the blade of a knife or bayonet. It is invariably fast and adrenalin fuelled. It epitomises the idea of 'hot courage', acting quickly in the mayhem of battle.

KAMAL RAM VC

12 May 1944

Painting by Henry Carr of Kamal Ram (1924–82) in the year he received his VC. Senior officers commented later that he had always been a superb soldier, even in training. (IWM, ART LD 4516)

Born in 1924 in a small village in Karauli State, India, Kamal Ram was one of three sons. His medal-winning action happened during his first engagement, when he was a sepoy. His age is officially given as 19, but as his birth date is not recorded he may have been as young as 15. His company of the 8th Punjab Regiment had crossed the River Gari in Italy overnight and were trying to secure a bridgehead when their advance was stopped by heavy machine gun fire from four posts to the front and sides. When the company commander asked for a volunteer to silence the right-hand post, Kamal Ram immediately stepped forward. He crawled through the wire and round the post, which he attacked single-handedly. He shot the first machine gunner, bayonetted the second, then shot a German officer who entered from the trench alongside the machine gun post. He then immediately moved to attack the second post on his own. He shot one machine gunner, and then threw in a grenade, causing the surviving crew to surrender. Kamal Ram then saw another soldier from his company scouting the third post, so he moved to join him. He covered his comrade's advance, then went in and completed the destruction of the third post. The company was then able to charge and secure the ground, so that the bridgehead could be established and work completed on two bridges.

George VI presents Ram his Victoria Cross in Italy, July 1944.

Later that day, a platoon widening the position came under fire from a house. Kamal Ram charged towards the house, shooting one German and capturing two others. His actions were integral to the success of the action, and crucial to his Battalion achieving their objective that day. He showed determination and aggression that would have been impressive in any soldier, but particularly impressive in a young soldier's first fire-fight.

For his actions he was awarded the Victoria Cross. He was presented with the ribbon by George VI in Italy in July 1944, and given the medal at an elaborate ceremony in Delhi later that year. After the Partition of India, Ram moved to the Rajput Regiment, where he held the rank of Havildar. He later achieved the rank of Subedar. He died in 1982.

KAMAL RAM WAS THE YOUNGEST INDIAN VICTORIA CROSS RECIPIENT OF THE SECOND WORLD WAR.

WILLIAM GARDNER VC

5 May 1858

William Gardner (1821–97). This photograph was taken after the Crimean War, as one of a series of veteran portraits requested by Queen Victoria. (IWM, LI 2009 999 55 2, Courtesy of the Lord Ashcroft Collection)

Born in Lanarkshire, William Gardner joined the 42nd (Royal Highland) Regiment (later the Black Watch) as a young man. He served in the Crimea, and was at the siege of Sebastopol. He had been in the Army nearly 20 years when he fought in the Indian Mutiny.

On 5 May 1858, Colour-Sergeant Gardner's regiment were called on to support the 4th Punjab Rifles at the battle of Bareilly. The 4th Punjabis had been overpowered by mutineers, and were being pursued as they fell back towards the 42nd as they were forming up for the attack. The mass of fighting soldiers and mutineers, still fighting furiously, wheeled around the Regiment. As Gardner was moving along the rear of the troops, reloading his rifle, he saw Colonel Cameron, his commanding officer, being attacked by three mutineers. The men were dragging Cameron off his horse, and one was about to strike him when Gardner blocked the blow with his rifle. Gardner bayonetted the first attacker, then turned to the second. He recalled that:

> No. 2 then made a lunge at me with his sword. I guarded it in the same way. He also cut my rifle into the barrel, his sword, slipping down the rifle and just cut off the skin of my left thumb at the first joint. I then attacked No. 3 who had a large shield on his left arm. He was more cautious. He retired back and I was following him when some person shot him through the head … the whole affair did not occupy ½ minute, it was just as fast as I could put my bayonet in and pull it out again.

His swift and decisive actions saved the officer's life. For his action he was awarded the Victoria Cross, and he was invested with his medal in India in 1859. Later in the Mutiny he was second onto the walls at Lucknow at its final capture. In 1859 he was presented with a silver pocket watch by the NCOs and men of No. 5 Co 'as a token of their esteem and respect'. The NCO who presented it to him praised Gardner for his service and example saying: 'Your intrepidty, undaunted courage and daring bravery in the field has singled you out as a person worthy of the honour the queen has bestowed on you.'

The kukri that Gardner is said to have taken from one of the mutineers he fought off at Bareilly. (Courtesy of the Lord Ashcroft Collection)

After a distinguished career of 21 years, he was discharged in 1862, his papers noting his exemplary conduct. Returning to Scotland, he was appointed drill instructor of Bothwell Company, 2nd Lanarkshire Rifle Volunteers in 1864. On his retirement, after 21 years, he received a gold pocket watch, in recognition of 'his valued service as an instructor'.

When he died in 1897 his impressive funeral was attended by Crimea and Mutiny veterans, and representatives of both his regiments.

William Gardner's medal group. His descendants sold his medals to the Lord Ashcroft Collection in 2008 and gave the money to charity, notably a charity providing care for over 300 ex-servicemen and women throughout Scotland. (Courtesy of the Lord Ashcroft Collection)

ALBERT EDWARD McKENZIE VC

22–23 April 1918

Able Seaman Albert McKenzie (1898–1918). Born and raised in London, he was buried in Camberwell Cemetery. In 1919 a monument was erected over his grave. (IWM, A 152, by permission of Donald McKenzie)

Albert McKenzie, the youngest of a large family, joined the Royal Navy as a Boy First Class in 1913. In 1918, aged just 19, he volunteered to take part in the Zeebrugge raid. Bruges harbour was a base for German U-boats and Operation *Z-O* planned to block access to it by sinking old ships in the entrances to the canals at Zeebrugge and Ostend.

HMS *Vindictive*, along with two other ships, launched a diversionary attack on the mile-long Mole at Zeebrugge just after midnight on St George's Day, 23 April, while the other ships assumed position for the main attack. The landing was difficult and opposed by heavy fire from the Mole. McKenzie was part of the naval storming party commanded by Lieutenant-Commander Harrison. He landed on the Mole with his Lewis machine gun and ammunition and took part in a running fight against German positions. He advanced down the Mole with Harrison, and killed several German defenders who were running from a shelter to a destroyer moored beside the Mole. While working his gun, he was badly wounded in the back and the foot. He shot around 12 Germans before his gun was blown from his grasp. He then used the pistol grip to stun a German, giving him time to get out his pistol and finish him off. He continued to fight with his pistol despite his wounds until ordered to withdraw. McKenzie fought his way back to the ship using his pistol, a rifle and bayonet he found, and eventually his bare hands, pushing and kicking Germans out of his way until he was eventually pulled to safety. His wounds were so serious that he had to be carried back onto the *Vindictive*.

There was much rejoicing at the success of the Zeebrugge raid, and it was decided that recipients for the Victoria Cross would be selected from the raiders by ballot. In total seven Victoria Crosses were presented for the raid, four of them by ballot. McKenzie, who was being treated at the Royal Naval Hospital in Chatham at the time, was chosen by his fellow ratings to be one of the recipients. By the summer he was well enough to travel to London and was presented with his Victoria Cross at Buckingham Palace alongside the other Zeebrugge recipients on 31 July 1918.

McKenzie was still recovering from his wounds in hospital when he fell victim to the flu pandemic. He died one week before the Armistice, aged just 20. He was given a magnificent funeral, attended by fellow Zeebrugge Victoria Cross recipient, Captain Carpenter, and a message was read out from the king and queen.

McKenzie's action as depicted in the comic *The Victor*. (*The Victor* © D. C. Thomson & Co., Ltd)

GEORGE CARTWRIGHT VC

31 August 1918

George Cartwright (1894–1978) in 1918. (Australian War Memorial)

London-born George Cartwright emigrated to Australia in 1912 as an enterprising 18-year-old and worked at a sheep station in New South Wales. On his 21st birthday Cartwright enlisted in the Australian Imperial Force for service during the First World War. He became a private in the 33rd (New South Wales) Battalion, and arrived in France in November 1916.

He was first wounded in action in June 1917 at Messines, but remained on duty. In April 1918 he was one of a large number from the battalion who were victims of a concentrated German gas attack at Villers-Bretonneux. After hospitalisation he rejoined his unit in June.

At the beginning of the Hundred Days offensive, the Allies' great push which ultimately resulted in the Armistice, Cartwright and his unit were in the thick of the fighting, pushing forward nearly to Peronne by the end of August 1918. On 31 August, two companies were held up by enemy machine gun fire at the heavily defended Road Wood near Mont St Quentin. Heavy casualties were being taken by the Australians as they advanced, and it was proving

George Cartwright's medal group. (IWM, OMD 2387–2395)

impossible to dislodge the defenders. Under intense enemy fire, Cartwright stood up and attacked one of the most troublesome guns alone. He shot three of the crew, then bombed the post and captured the gun and nine other men. His quick and aggressive actions meant that the advance could continue, and his battalion stood up and cheered him before resuming the attack with vigour. For his actions he was awarded the Victoria Cross. He miraculously came through this ordeal unscathed, but in the battles for the Hindenburg Line he was wounded on 30 September and evacuated to England.

Having received his Victoria Cross from George V at Buckingham Palace on 8 March 1919, Cartwright returned to Australia. Between the wars he settled into civilian life, but never lost his love for Army life. He joined the Citizen Force in 1932, and was mobilised for full-time service in 1940. He performed training and other duties in Australia until he was placed on the Retired List after the war. He travelled from Australia to London for the Victoria Cross centenary celebrations in 1956, and later reunions of the Victoria Cross and George Cross Association. He died in 1978, and his widow carried out his wishes by presenting his medals to the Imperial War Museum. His is one of only a handful of Australian VCs to be held outside of Australia.

The German Maxim heavy machine gun that Cartwright took in Road Wood. (Australian War Memorial)

'Pte George Cartwright, in the face of the most withering fire, stood up and advanced, firing his rifle from the shoulder.'
Lt-Col L J Morshead, Cartwright's commanding officer

EDWARD MANNOCK VC

1918

Edward Mannock (1887–1918). Though there has been some dispute about Mannock's score of 73 victories, as he only claimed 51 himself, he is without doubt one of the highest-scoring British aces, if not the highest. (Topfoto)

The son of an Irish soldier, Edward Mannock spent several years of his childhood abroad. While in India, he suffered temporary blindness, which permanently damaged his left eye. While he was still a boy, his father abandoned the family and Mannock was forced to leave school to help support the family.

When the First World War began he was working in Turkey, and he was interned as a British national. Due to his ill-treatment, Mannock became very sick and was eventually repatriated back to England. Despite his ill-health and poor eyesight, he rejoined the territorial unit of the Royal Army Medical Corps that he served in before the war. But following his experiences in Turkey he was determined to fight. He joined the Royal Engineers, then started pilot training, cheating to pass his sight test.

Having completed his training, Mannock reported to 40 Squadron in Treizennes, France, in April 1917. Older than many of the other pilots, he did not make a good first impression. But his persistence and determination began to show through, and the other pilots started to warm to him. In June he scored his first confirmed victory, and soon his victories began to mount up. In July he was awarded the Military Cross, promoted to captain and given command of a flight. After initial mistakes, he became an excellent patrol leader, determined to look after the members of his flight especially new pilots.

Mannock was now becoming expert at destroying enemy two-seaters, downing six in September, when he was awarded a bar to his Military Cross.

In January 1918, after 16 confirmed victories, Mannock left 40 Squadron and the front line. A short while later, however, he was posted as a Flight Commander to 74 Squadron and in late March, the squadron left for St Omer, France. Mannock only served in 74 Squadron for three months, but in that time he scored 33 victories alone, shared in three more, and probably accounted for many more. In May he was awarded the DSO, and over the following weeks, a further two bars to it.

'Old lad, if I am killed I shall be in good company. I feel I have done my duty.'
Edward Mannock to Ira Jones before his final flight

Mannock's dog tags were anonymously returned to his family from Germany after the war, along with his pocket notebook and revolver. His grave has never been found. (IWM LI 2009 999 55 3 2, Courtesy of the Lord Ashcroft Collection)

By now his nerves were badly affected and he became increasingly obsessed with the idea of being shot down in flames. Nonetheless his score continued to rise. In early July 1918, Mannock, now a major, took command of 85 Squadron. He worked hard to improve morale and tactics, transforming the spirit in the squadron within weeks, and adding eight to his own score. But he confided in friends that he did not think he would last much longer.

On 26 July 1918, Mannock took up a new pilot, Lieutenant Donald Inglis, to help him achieve his first victory. After they downed a two-seater, Mannock unusually circled the burning wreck twice, a tactic which opened them up to the enemy. As they turned for the British lines, Mannock was hit by German ground fire, and crashed in flames. Attempts to identify the wreck from the air were unsuccessful, and Mannock's body was not recovered. His grave was never identified, although his personal effects were returned from Germany after the war. The pilots of 74 and 85 squadrons were stunned by the death of Mannock, one of the greatest Allied fighter pilots and also an exemplary leader.

After the war, Mannock's friends and comrades were determined that his bravery and leadership should not go unrecognised, and their campaign to have him posthumously awarded the Victoria Cross finally achieved success in July 1919. His citation mentioned seven instances of his aggressive attacks on German aircraft, and concluded: 'This highly distinguished officer, during the whole of his career in the Royal Air Force, was an outstanding example of fearless courage, remarkable skill, devotion to duty and self-sacrifice, which has never been surpassed.'

'He moulded us into a team, and because of his skilled leadership we became a highly efficient team. Our squadron leader said that Mannock was the most skilful patrol leader in World War I, which would account for the relatively few casualties in his flight team compared with the high number of enemy aircraft destroyed.'
H. G. Clements, 74 Squadron, 1981

Mannock's gallantry medals. Mannock's father, long estranged from the family, and specifically excluded from Mannock's will, was presented with his son's medals. He then disappeared again, and it was many years before he was found and Mannock's medals given to his brother. (Courtesy of the Lord Ashcroft Collection)

ABDUL HAFIZ VC

6 April 1944

Abdul Hafiz (1915–44). Hafiz was buried near Imphal, then later moved to the Imphal Indian Army War Cemetery. (IWM, IND 3508)

Abdul Hafiz's widow receiving his Victoria Cross. She was pregnant when her husband died, and so he never met his daughter. (IWM, IND 3974)

Abdul Hafiz was born in 1915 in the Punjab and in 1944 was a Jemadar in the 9th Jat Infantry, part of the Anglo-Indian force tasked with stopping the determined Japanese attempts to invade India. During the battle of Imphal in 1944, around 40 Japanese troops occupied high ground overlooking a Jat company position, ten miles north of the city. On 6 April, the company commander ordered Jemadar Abdul Hafiz to attack the position with two sections from his platoon. Before the attack Hafiz addressed his men, assuring them that they were invincible and that all the enemy on the hill would be killed or put to flight. He then led his men from the front, and due to his rousing words, and the example of his leadership, the assault hit hard from the start. Tirelessly they attacked up the completely exposed slope towards the well-defended Japanese positions. The slope was steepest just before the crest, and as they tackled it they came under heavy attack from machine guns and grenades. As he reached the top Hafiz was wounded in the leg, but despite his injuries he dashed towards a Japanese machine gun, which was causing severe casualties, and forced the barrel up while a fellow soldier killed the enemy gunner. Hafiz then took a Bren gun from a wounded comrade and advanced against the Japanese, firing from the hip as he moved. His citation states that 'So fierce was that attack, and all his men so inspired by the determination of Jemadar Abdul Hafiz to kill all enemy in sight at whatever cost, that the enemy, who were still in considerable numbers on the position, ran down the opposite slope of the hill.'

Machine gun fire was now incoming from another position and as Hafiz continued to pursue the fleeing Japanese, he was mortally wounded in the chest. He collapsed but tried to continue firing the Bren gun and shouting orders and encouragement to his men. He died shortly afterwards. He had led the attack with such aggression that the position was carried against the odds with Japanese casualties alone far outnumbering the attackers. The Japanese had retreated so swiftly that Hafiz's comrades were even able to recover a number of weapons from the summit. The brave actions of Hafiz and his comrades played a small but significant part in the eventual Japanese defeat at Imphal, a major turning point in the Burma campaign.

The announcement was made on 27 July that Hafiz had been posthumously awarded the Victoria Cross. His medal was presented to his widow, Jugri Begum, by the Viceroy, Field Marshal Lord Wavell in October 1944 at a grand ceremony at the Red Fort in Delhi.

HAFIZ WAS THE FIRST MUSLIM OFFICER OF THE INDIAN ARMY TO BE AWARDED THE VICTORIA CROSS.

CHARLES JOHN STANLEY GOUGH VC
15 & 18 August 1857, 27 January & 28 February 1858

Charles Gough (1832–1912). (IWM, Q 80525)

Charles Gough about to strike the mutineer threatening his brother at Khurkowdah in August 1857. (National Army Museum)

Charles John Stanley Gough was born in India but grew up in Ireland. The Gough family were a military family with long-standing connections to India. When Gough was 16 he returned to India and joined the 8th Bengal Cavalry, serving in the Second Anglo-Sikh War in 1848–49.

Following the outbreak of the Indian Mutiny the Bengal Army was brought into the British Army and by the age of 25 Gough was a major in the 5th Bengal European Cavalry. During the Indian Mutiny he fought with several units in a variety of engagements, including the siege and capture of Delhi, the first relief of Lucknow, and the capture of Lucknow. The actions of this dashing and courageous cavalry officer were particularly noted on four occasions.

On 15 August, at the battle of Khurkowdah near Rhotuck, he was in the thick of the fighting, when his younger brother Hugh was wounded. Charles saved his brother from a mutineer and went on to kill two of the enemy. Hugh would also receive the Victoria Cross for two instances of valour during the Indian Mutiny.

On 18 August, Charles Gough led a troop of the Guide cavalry in a charge, and cut down two enemy cavalrymen, one after desperate hand-to-hand combat. The following January, at the battle of Shumshabad, Gough attacked a mutineer leader, running him through with his sword. His sword being lodged in the body of the mutineer, Gough was surrounded by the enemy with only his revolver, but he continued to fight, shooting two of the enemy. The next month, at the attack on the fort of Meeangunge, he assisted Brevet Major O. H. St George Anson by charging a mutineer who was about to attack with drawn sword, killing him with a powerful blow to the head. He then immediately cut down another mutineer in the same manner.

For his valour on these four occasions, and many others, when he aggressively fought mutineers in hand-to-hand combat, defending positions and saving lives, he was recommended for the Victoria Cross.

After the Indian Mutiny Gough continued his career in the Army. He had command of an infantry brigade during the Second Anglo-Afghan War, inflicting a crushing defeat on the enemy at Futtehabad in 1879, and leading the column to relieve the siege of the Sherpur Cantonment in 1880. He was knighted in 1881, and ten years later became a full general.

He retired to Ireland in 1895, being made Knight Grand Cross of the Order of the Bath the same year. Gough and his wife had six children. One of his sons, John, received the Victoria Cross for his actions in Somaliland in 1903. Another son, Hubert, commanded the British Fifth Army from 1916–18.

THE GOUGHS CAN BE CONSIDERED BRITAIN'S BRAVEST FAMILY, AS THEY ARE UNIQUE IN BEING AWARDED THREE VICTORIA CROSSES.

EDWARD BENN SMITH VC

21–23 August 1918

Edward Benn Smith (1898–1940). A noted rugby player and boxer, Smith never married. (IWM, VC 6164)

Ned Smith grew up in a small coastal town in Cumbria. When he turned 18, in 1917, he left his job as a coal miner and joined the Lancashire Fusiliers. He was posted to the 1/5th Battalion, and arrived in France later that year. Smith was aged only 19 when the Hundred Days offensive began in 1918. On 10 August, at Hébuterne during the battle of Amiens, Smith was leading a daylight patrol when he saw around 40 Germans who were moving to a position away from the German front lines, to begin outpost duty. Despite being outnumbered ten to one, Smith led his men against the enemy, causing heavy casualties, before withdrawing without any losses of his own. For this action he received the Distinguished Conduct Medal and was promoted to Lance Sergeant.

Later that month, Smith was in command of a platoon east of Serre. He personally captured a machine gun post, armed with just his rifle and bayonet. As he approached, the enemy scattered to throw grenades at him, but almost without halting, Smith shot and killed at least six of them, helping another platoon take their objective. Later that day, he saw that another platoon needed assistance, and led his men to help them, once again taking command and capturing the objective. The following day, during a German counter-attack, he led a section forward and restored a portion of the line. In just a few days he had shown great personal determination, and also taken command in two situations that required firm leadership by example.

His actions would have been impressive in any soldier, but for a young man of 19, who had been in the Army less than a year, it was remarkable. He was awarded the Victoria Cross, which was presented to him by George V at Buckingham Palace in November 1918. At the time he was the youngest Victoria Cross holder in the Army. When he returned home in 1919, he was greeted by a cheering crowd of 6,000, the size of the entire population of his home town.

Having survived the war unscathed, Smith chose to make the Army his career, serving in China, Malaya and Ireland, until he retired in 1938, as Regimental Sergeant Major, after 21 years service.

In summer 1939, as war seemed inevitable, he re-joined his old regiment, the Lancashire Fusiliers, and was in the first contingent of the 2nd British Expeditionary Force to sail for France. Smith knew that he was going to have to defend almost the same ground he had fought for over 20 years previously. On 12 January 1940, he shot himself.

Edward Benn Smith's medal group. (Courtesy of the Lord Ashcroft Collection)

LEADERSHIP

'by force of example and inspiring leadership'

Charismatic, strong, inspirational, the natural leader not only takes command, but also infuses all those around them with confidence and hope. They exude calm and resolve. They are a tower of strength. Like a steadily flowing wave, strong Leadership washes away the dam until the tide flows again where previously the waters were still.

ALFRED BLAKENEY CARPENTER VC

22–23 April 1918

Alfred Blakeney Carpenter was born in Barnes, Surry, into a naval family. He joined the Royal Navy as a cadet in 1896. By the beginning of the First World War he was an experienced officer specialising in navigation and was serving in the battleship HMS *Iron Duke* on the staff of Admiral Sir John Jellicoe, the Commander-in-Chief of the Grand Fleet. He was promoted to commander and appointed navigating commander on HMS *Emperor of India*.

In 1917, Carpenter was taken onto the staff of Vice-Admiral Roger Keyes, who was the new director of plans at the Admiralty. Carpenter was involved in the secret planning for the attacks on Zeebrugge and Ostend, which aimed to block the entrances to the German submarine base at Bruges. Carpenter was delighted to be given the command of HMS *Vindictive*, an old cruiser chosen to lead the raid on Zeebrugge.

The *Vindictive* was tasked with a diversionary attack on Zeebrugge's fortified Mole, while three blocking ships, loaded with concrete, manoeuvred into position in the entrance to the canal and scuttled themselves. Carpenter's first task was to lead the fleet across the Channel, without lights or radio. He then had to carefully navigate *Vindictive* through mined waters. As the ship approached the fortified Mole, the German defenders directed heavy fire at the ship, much of it concentrated on the bridge. Despite this Carpenter remained calm and cool. He brought the ship alongside the Mole, an

Alfred Blakeney Carpenter (centre) (1881–1955). In 1913 he was awarded the silver medal of the Royal Humane Society for saving life at sea, as was his father before him. (IWM, Q 20831)

extraordinarily difficult task in the darkness and under fire. With the *Vindictive* in position, Carpenter supervised the landings and directed operations, encouraging the men, all from a dangerously exposed position. As the operation ended, the *Vindictive* was hit by an enemy shell. Carpenter was badly wounded, but he stayed in command, waiting ten minutes after the withdrawal signal until the wounded were aboard, before allowing the *Vindictive* to leave. He then brought the *Vindictive* away safely under intense German shelling.

Carpenter's cap was damaged by gunfire during the raid. (IWM, UNI 908)

This is the whistle that Carpenter used to give the signal to storm the Mole during the Zeebrugge raid. He was just 36 when he commanded the *Vindictive* at Zeebrugge, and was promoted to acting captain for the operation. (IWM, EPH 10132)

The 'Vindictive' at Zeebrugge: the storming of Zeebrugge Mole by Charles J. de Lacy. Carpenter admitted later that he had put the ship 300 yards further along the Mole than planned, as it was difficult to recognise objects in the dark and under fire. (IWM, ART 871)

Such an audacious and complicated operation could only have succeeded if every man stuck to his task, remaining focussed and calm. In his first dispatch, Admiral Keyes commented that Carpenter's composure and bravery had encouraged similar behaviour in his crew.

Carpenter was the senior surviving officer and after the raid he was asked to make recommendations for conspicuous gallantry, but he refused to select individuals as he felt all had served bravely. Instead, recipients for the Victoria Cross were chosen by ballot. Carpenter chose not to vote. However, he was the choice of the officers of the *Vindictive*, *Iris II* and *Daffodil*, the supporting vessels on the operation, and of the entire naval assaulting force. He received his Victoria Cross in July 1918 with the other Zeebrugge recipients and was immediately confirmed in his promotion to captain. He later received the Croix de Guerre, and the Légion d'Honneur. After the war, Carpenter held land and sea commands, and staff appointments. In 1921, he published a book titled *The Blocking of Zeebrugge*. He was promoted rear admiral in 1929, and retired shortly after.

During his retirement he helped introduce the idea of a training ship for cadets and junior officers of the Merchant Navy, and for most of the Second World War he was commanding officer of his local Home Guard battalion. In 1945 he became Director of Shipping at the Admiralty. He died peacefully at home aged 74.

The case for Carpenter's binoculars showing shrapnel damage suffered during the raid. (IWM, OPT 543)

Augustus Charles Newman VC

27 March 1942

Charles Newman (1904–72). Before Operation *Chariot* Newman was told that married men with families could withdraw because it was so dangerous. Newman himself had four children, and his wife was expecting their fifth, but he chose to go. (IWM, HU 16542)

In 1942, Lieutenant Colonel Newman was chosen to lead the commandos in one of the most daring raids of the Second World War. St Nazaire was the only port large enough to service the German battleship *Tirpitz* on the French coast. The purpose of the raid was to destroy the dry dock and so prevent its use by the *Tirpitz*, Germany's largest battleship, referred to by Churchill as 'the beast'. To do this, the destroyer HMS *Cambeltown* would be blown up across the dock gates. At the same time, Newman and his men, mainly from No.2 Commando, were to destroy dock installations, bridges and two flak towers. It was an extremely dangerous operation, with little chance of the men returning.

Before reaching the harbour, the attack party had to travel 5 miles up the Loire River. Caught by searchlights, they came under heavy cross-fire. Ignoring the bullets, Newman stood coolly in the leading craft. Newman had been authorised to call off the mission at any point, but even when bomber support had to be abandoned due to the weather, he remained determined to see it through. He was one of the first off the landing craft and for the next five hours he led the bitter fighting. He personally entered and cleared several sniper-occupied houses, supervised operations in the town, and directed fire, regardless of his own safety.

Under his leadership the troops held back superior forces until the demolition teams had done their work. But by now, most of landing craft had sunk or were on fire. Newman wanted to give the surviving commandos, many of them wounded, the best possible chance of escape, and so he tried to break out of the town to open country. Divided into small groups, the men made their way towards safety. Though wounded in the stomach himself, Newman led a fighting retreat of around 15 wounded men out of the harbour over a narrow, defended bridge into the town. They fought through the streets of the town, but were then overpowered when out of ammunition. Newman spent the rest of the war in a prisoner-of-war camp.

His 'brilliant leadership' was largely responsible for the commandos' success during the raid but his Victoria Cross was announced following his repatriation after the war when accounts were given of the raid. His was one of five Victoria Crosses awarded to the raiders. Newman was also decorated with the Légion d'Honneur and the Croix de Guerre but despite this recognition, he remained modest remarking, 'I always felt I got my gong for the operation, not for what I did myself. I'm nothing special and it's silly that I should be regarded as such.'

The commandos at St Nazaire, painting by David Rowlands. The fighting was bitter and of the 600 men involved in the raid, around two-thirds were captured or killed. (© David Rowlands)

JOHN WALLACE LINTON VC

1939–43

John Wallace Linton (1905–43). A skilled mathematician, he received the second maths prize at the Royal Naval College Dartmouth. He also loved rugby, even having trials for England. Linton acquired the nickname 'Tubby' after giving up rugby. (Courtesy of The Royal Navy Submarine Museum, Gosport)

John Linton attended the Royal Naval College Dartmouth and entered the submarine service in 1927. He would stay in submarines almost exclusively for the rest of his life, becoming one of the greatest Allied submariner commanders.

Linton was commanding HMS *Pandora* when the Second World War broke out. In May 1940 he took the *Pandora* on its first war patrol in the Aegean. By May 1941, he had completed 11 Mediterranean combat patrols, and had received a DSC for sinking two Italian supply ships in one attack. After leaving *Pandora* in May he chose to stay in operational submarine command, instead of accepting a training or staff appointment. He commissioned the new T-class submarine, HMS *Turbulent*, later that year and became her first, and only, commanding officer.

HMS *Turbulent* joined the 1st Submarine Flotilla at Alexandria in February 1942. Commander Linton's skill and aggression in attack were borne out by his spectacular results. Under Linton's command *Turbulent* destroyed around 100,000 tons of shipping, including a cruiser, a destroyer, a U-boat and even, remarkably, three trains thanks to his aggressive use of the submarine's guns.

In September 1942, Linton received the DSO for four Mediterranean patrols. By this time, 'Tubby' Linton was the oldest and most experienced commander in the flotilla, frequently a source of advice for younger captains.

February 1943 saw *Turbulent* sail on her tenth, and Linton's 21st, patrol; his last patrol before he took some well-deserved leave.

John Linton's medal group. In February 1944, Linton's VC and DSO were presented to his eldest son William, then a naval cadet. William was tragically lost at sea seven years later. (Courtesy of the Lord Ashcroft Collection)

HMS *Turbulent* was last seen on around 12 March. No messages were received from her after this time. In early May, the captain and crew were posted missing, presumed killed. *Turbulent* probably hit a mine off Sardinia, but the wreck has never been found, her loss with all hands remains a mystery to this day.

On 25 May, a Victoria Cross was gazetted for Linton. Unusually, this was for his sustained period of gallant leadership over nearly four years rather than a single action like most VCs. He had spent an incredible 254 days of his last year at sea, submerged for nearly half the time. During this time *Turbulent* was hunted 13 times, and depth-charged 250 times.

The citation relates in detail the occasion when he sighted a convoy of two merchantmen and two Italian destroyers at night. He moved in front of the convoy, and dived to attack it as the silhouettes of the ships moved through the moon's rays. Bringing his sights to bear, he realised he was in the path of one of the destroyers, but he held his course until it was almost on top of him. When the convoy were in sights, he fired. He sank two of the ships outright, and one blew up.

'... his many brilliant successes were due to his constant activity, skill, and daring which never failed him when there was an enemy to be attacked.'
London Gazette, 25 May 1943

WALTER RICHARD POLLOCK HAMILTON VC

2 April 1879

Walter Hamilton (1856–79). He was born in County Kilkenny in 1856. (IWM, W 173631)

Described as over six feet tall, of fine appearance, and devoted to his men, Walter Hamilton was the epitome of the Victorian British officer. At the age of 18, he joined the 70th (Surrey) Regiment and was posted to India. In 1876 he was promoted to full lieutenant and received a commission in the Queen's Own Corps of Guides.

During the Second Anglo-Afghan War, Hamilton served with the Guides cavalry. At the battle of Futtehabad on 2 April 1879, the Guides cavalry were ordered to charge after the enemy had been drawn out. During the charge, the commander of the Guides was shot and killed. Hamilton was the only officer left. He immediately took command, urging the men to avenge their commander's death. The cavalry swept into the enemy position and the Afghan forces fled. During the battle a sowar, an Indian cavalry soldier, fell from his horse and was attacked by three of the enemy. Hamilton cut down the attackers, saving the man's life. For these actions, Hamilton was recommended for the Victoria Cross.

The summer of 1879 saw the British withdrawing from Afghanistan following the treaty of Gandamak. Hamilton remained behind in Kabul, as military attaché to the resident British envoy, and in command of the envoy's escort. In September, the mission was attacked by thousands of mutinous Afghan soldiers. Appeals to the Amir for help went unanswered. The mission was indefensible, but Hamilton did his best to fortify it, and he and his 70 Guides put up a heroic defence, holding off a much larger force for eight long hours. When the Afghans brought up two guns against the mission Hamilton knew they were doomed unless they could seize the guns. He and his men made three valiant attempts to take the guns but on the last attempt they were so few in number they could only target one gun. When they reached it, Hamilton told his men to get the gun back to the building while he held off the attackers. He fought heroically, but was overwhelmed and cut to pieces. He was just 23. The handful of Guides still standing fought to the last man in the burning embassy.

The recommendation for Hamilton's Victoria Cross had initially been turned down as his action was similar to other recent awards, but after further discussion it was sanctioned in September by which time he had already been killed at Kabul. It was back-dated to ensure it did not set a precedent of posthumous awards. However if posthumous awards had been allowed at this time, Hamilton might well have become the first recipient of a bar to the Victoria Cross for his actions at Kabul.

M.M. Kaye, the wife of one of his descendants, published a best-selling novel, *The Far Pavilions*, in 1978. This opus featured Walter Hamilton, and brought his actions to an audience of over 15 million.

The damaged silver watch found on Hamilton's burned body. The inscription reads: 'Burned on the body of Lt. Walter Pollock Hamilton, VC. Aged 23 at Kabul. 3rd September 1879.' (IWM, LI 2009 999 64 3 3, Courtesy of the Lord Ashcroft Collection)

Hamilton's sword was also retrieved from his body after his death in Kabul. (IWM, LI 2009 999 64 3 1, Courtesy of the Lord Ashcroft Collection)

Geoffrey Heneage Drummond VC

9–10 May 1918

As a child, Drummond dislocated his neck in an accident, which left him a semi-invalid. He managed to work, and sail, but suffered many debilitating headaches. After the First World War broke out, Drummond underwent treatment in hopes of serving his country, and joined the Royal Naval Volunteer Reserve in 1915. In 1918, Drummond was a lieutenant commanding *Motor Launch 254* at Dover. During the first Ostend raid on 23 April, Drummond was involved in laying down the smoke screen. He was mentioned in dispatches and promoted.

Two weeks later, he was in action again, having volunteered for the second raid on Ostend on the night of 9–10 May. *ML254* was one of five motor launches attached to the raid. The plan called for the motor launches to follow the block ships HMS *Vindictive* and HMS *Sappho* into the harbour and, once they had scuttled themselves, take off any surviving crew. The raid did not start well, as HMS *Sappho* was forced to abandon the mission

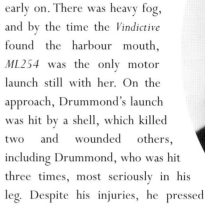

Geoffrey Drummond (1886–1941). His father was a Rifle Brigade officer, and Drummond was educated at Eton and Christ Church, Oxford. (IWM, Q 79805)

The jacket that Drummond was wearing during the Ostend raid, bloodstained and ripped, especially on the right shoulder. (IWM, UNI 13788)

early on. There was heavy fog, and by the time the *Vindictive* found the harbour mouth, *ML254* was the only motor launch still with her. On the approach, Drummond's launch was hit by a shell, which killed two and wounded others, including Drummond, who was hit three times, most seriously in his leg. Despite his injuries, he pressed on, showing considerable skill in bringing the motor launch alongside the *Vindictive* after it had run aground. He took off 38 crew and two officers, then managed to back out of the harbour, all under heavy fire. The launch had been badly damaged, and, weighed down with the survivors of *Vindictive*, it was close to sinking. Finally having got the launch clear from the harbour, Drummond collapsed from his wounds. Drummond's actions undoubtedly saved the lives of 40 men, and would have been remarkable enough even had he not been seriously wounded, and his launch badly damaged. For his determination and courage he was awarded the Victoria Cross. He received his decoration from George V alongside the two other Ostend VCs on 11 September 1918.

Drummond stayed with the RNVR until November 1919. After leaving, he had trouble finding work, eventually joining ICI. In 1939, Drummond tried to rejoin the RNVR, but was rejected due to his age and ill-health. Instead he enlisted in the Thames River Patrol Service as an ordinary seaman. In 1941, while awaiting a commission, he fell while loading coal and sustained a fractured skull, from which he later died.

GORDON MURIEL FLOWERDEW VC

30 March 1918

George Flowerdew (1885–1918).
(IWM, VC 416)

Gordon Flowerdew was born in Norfolk, one of 14 children, and emigrated to Canada aged 18 to work as a rancher. In Canada, he joined a militia regiment and following the outbreak of the First World War, he transferred to Lord Strathcona's Horse. Posted to the Western Front, he saw his first action in 1915. His wartime diary records his hopes of receiving the Victoria Cross one day. He was commissioned as an officer in 1916, and took part in the bloody fighting on the Somme and around Cambrai. By early 1918 he was a highly experienced junior officer in command of C Squadron.

In March 1918, the German spring offensive was creating a gap between the British and French forces near Amiens. The Canadian Cavalry Brigade were part of the force ordered to seal this gap at Bois de Moreuil. On 30 March, they moved to engage and delay the enemy. Under Lieutenant Flowerdew, the 75-strong C Squadron was detached to attack Germans entering the wood at the north-east corner. Flowerdew led his men around the northern end of the wood, where he came upon 60 Germans in two lines, heavily armed with machine guns. He detached a dismounted troop to outflank the enemy, then brought the other three troops into line, and charged with sabres drawn. The charge went through both lines, killing many of the enemy with their swords, then wheeled around and galloped on them again. They managed to dislodge the Germans, even though they suffered an appalling casualty rate of 70 per cent. After scattering the enemy, the survivors then re-formed in the wood, and joined by the dismounted troop, they fought hand-to-hand until they had captured their area of the wood, and destroyed the German garrison. During the fighting, Flowerdew was seriously wounded, but continued to cheer and encourage his men from where he lay. His tactical decision to split his men, and his leadership, including his encouragement while lying wounded, were vital to the success of the action.

Flowerdew had been shot through both thighs. One leg was amputated, but he died the next day. Before he died he was told that he had been recommended for the Victoria Cross he so desired.

Flowerdew's heroic charge is feted as the 'Last Great Cavalry Charge' and is one of the most famous incidents in the Regiment's history. Brigadier-General Seely, commander of the Canadian Cavalry Brigade, said that Flowerdew 'played a wonderful part in the greatest battle in history'. Flowerdew's posthumous Victoria Cross was given to his mother by the king in July 1918.

The charge of Flowerdew's squadron, painted by Alfred Mullings. (Beaverbrook Collection of War Art, © Canadian War Museum)

THOMAS WILKINSON VC

14 February 1942

Thomas Wilkinson (1898–1942). He went to sea at 14, joining his father's ship. During the First World War he served in the Merchant Navy. (IWM, A 31245)

A model of the *Li Wo* which was presented to the Imperial War Museum in 1951 by representatives of the Indo-China Steam Navigation Company and the Hong Kong and Whampoa Dock Company in memory of her gallant action. (IWM, MOD 408)

Thomas Wilkinson was born in Lancashire, the youngest of five sons in a seafaring family. In the early 1920s, Wilkinson joined the Indo-China Steam Navigation Company. In 1938, he became skipper of the *Li Wo*, a small flat-bottomed passenger steamer designed for use on the upper Yangtze River.

When the Second World War broke out, the *Li Wo* was taken over by the Royal Navy as a patrol vessel, and given a 4in gun, two machine guns, and a depth-charge thrower. Wilkinson became a temporary Lieutenant in the Royal Naval Reserve. HMS *Li Wo* left the safety of the Yangtze and put to sea. Arriving in Singapore a few days before the city fell to the Japanese, Wilkinson received orders to go on to Batavia (now Jakarta), Indonesia. The *Li Wo*, carrying 84 officers and men, left Singapore on 13 February 1941. They were attacked several times by Japanese bombers, then at 4pm the next day, a convoy of small ships appeared, followed by a second convoy of larger Imperial Japanese Navy vessels, accompanied by a heavy cruiser and a destroyer. There was no way out for the river boat. Wilkinson told the ship's company they would not try to escape, but would fight to the last in hopes of causing damage. They all supported his decision even though the 4in gun had just 13 shells remaining.

Though small, the *Li Wo* was highly manoeuvrable. Wilkinson brought the ship around and steamed straight at one of the Japanese transports.

A scratch crew manned the gun and landed a direct hit on the transport, which began to burn. Over the next hour, fire rained in from the Japanese warships causing many casualties, and dealing the ship critical damage, but regardless they continued towards the transport, returning fire with their machine guns. Wilkinson rammed the transport, hoping to sink it before the *Li Wo* sank. He managed to rip a gaping hole in the transport, causing it to sink the next day. However, a cruiser had now closed in on them, and they had run out of ammunition. One last salvo from the cruiser decided their fate.

Wilkinson ordered the surviving company to abandon ship. The Japanese machine guns continued to fire at the survivors as they tried to escape. Wilkinson remained on the bridge and went down with the ship, its battle ensign flying as it disappeared beneath the waves.

Eventually, around ten men from the *Li Wo* made it to land, where they were later taken prisoner. Seven survived the war, and returned home to tell the story of the *Li Wo*. In 1946, more than ten awards were made to those who had been on the *Li Wo*, making her the most decorated small ship in the Royal Navy. Wilkinson was awarded a posthumous Victoria Cross 'in recognition both of his own heroism and self-sacrifice and of that of all who fought and died with him'.

THE CAPTAIN OF THE *MOST DECORATED SMALL SHIP* IN THE ROYAL NAVY.

DEREK ANTHONY SEAGRIM VC
20–21 March 1943
HUGH PAUL SEAGRIM GC
February 1943–September 1944

Derek Seagrim (1903–43). He and his brothers grew up in their father's rural parish. When Derek first took command of 7th Battalion, Green Howards, the men were not sure what to make of him, assuming that his staff background meant he had spent years behind a desk, but he soon showed his mettle. (IWM, HU 1998)

Hugh Seagrim (1909–44). He was a well-liked officer who played football in the regimental team and was considered clever, eccentric and delightful. (IWM, HU 66776)

Derek and Hugh Seagrim were the middle and youngest of five soldiering brothers, born into a family steeped in military history. After the Royal Military College, Sandhurst, Derek was commissioned into the Green Howards in 1923. Hugh originally wanted to become a doctor, but when his father died it was no longer possible for him to go to university. Not wanting to follow his brothers, he tried to join the Royal Navy. He was rejected due to his colour-blindness, so followed two of his brothers to Sandhurst.

By the beginning of the Second World War, Derek was an experienced officer who had served around the world. During the early part of the war he held several staff appointments. He then was given command of the 7th Battalion, Green Howards at El Alamein in the North African desert with the rank of temporary lieutenant-colonel.

On the night of 20 March 1943, after advancing west across Libya, the 7th Battalion were tasked with capturing a key feature on the Mareth Line, on the left flank of the main attack. They immediately came under intense fire, from machine guns, artillery and mortars, and started taking heavy casualties. It was crucial to the main attack that they capture the feature so Derek led the attack from the front, completely disregarding the constant barrage of enemy fire. Coming to an anti-tank ditch, Derek helped place the first scaling ladder over it, and was the first to cross. Later, two machine gun posts were holding up one of his companies, so he personally assaulted them, one after the other, killing and capturing 20 German soldiers. His courageous leadership directly led to the capture of the bastion. The battalion then had to hold the position under intense fire and against determined German counter-attacks throughout the next day. Derek moved from post to post, encouraging his men and directing fire until all the attackers were wiped out. Led by his example, the battalion held the feature, enabling the main attack to be carried out. For his actions he was awarded the Victoria Cross, though he did not live to receive it as he died in early April from wounds sustained at the battle of Wadi Akarit.

After Sandhurst, Hugh Seagrim was commissioned into the Burma Rifles. Remarkably, he passed his examination in spoken Burmese in just five weeks. He travelled during periods of leave, and got to know Burma and its people very well, in particular the Karens, Burmese hill people.

In 1941, after the start of the war with Japan, Hugh was tasked with raising guerrilla forces in Burma to attack the Japanese Army. The Japanese advance into Burma was so swift that he did not have much time to organise the resistance, but when the British retreated into India he chose to stay behind with the Karens, working alone and unsupported in the hills and villages, at constant risk of capture. Major Seagrim, his 6ft 4in frame dressed in Karen clothes, became a legend in Burma, known as Hpu Taw Kaw,

Derek Seagrim leading his men across the anti-tank ditch, which was 8ft deep and 12ft wide, surrounded by minefields. (The National Archives)

Despite this, the Karens continued to assist Hugh. Eventually the Japanese got a message to Hugh that they would stop their actions against the Karens if he surrendered. Knowing the Japanese would probably kill him, Hugh walked into a Japanese camp in March 1944 and surrendered to stop the reprisals. He was imprisoned in Rangoon with eight of his men. Even his Japanese captors came to respect Hugh as he comforted his men during months of captivity.

On 2 September, Hugh was sentenced to death. He pleaded that his men be spared from execution, yet the Karens insisted they wanted to die with him. They were all beheaded. For his bravery working undercover, his self-sacrifice in handing himself in, and his pleading for the lives of his men, he was awarded a posthumous George Cross. He is still remembered with fondness by the Karens today.

'Grandfather Long Legs'. Though undertaken deep within enemy territory, his tireless work against the Japanese was recognised: he was made MBE in 1942 and in 1943, a DSO was dropped in with his supplies. He managed to recruit a thousand-strong irregular army, to help lost units get back to India, and assist the British when they returned.

In 1943, two British officers and some Karen volunteers made contact with Seagrim, and the group ran intelligence and resistance in the hills for months. Late in the year, the Japanese discovered that they were operating in the area. They tried to bribe and threaten the Karens to betray them, without success. In February 1944 the two British officers were ambushed and killed, but Hugh continued to evade capture.

The Japanese started a campaign of attrition, destroying Karen villages and arresting at least 270 people, many of whom were tortured or killed.

Mrs Seagrim and her five sons. Derek is far right, with Hugh next to him. The newspapers reporting Hugh's George Cross stated that the combined service of the five brothers totalled nearly 100 years. When Mrs Seagrim collected her youngest son's posthumous award for gallantry, she still had two sons in active service, and one son invalided home. (Reproduced by kind permission of the Seagrim family)

DEREK SEAGRIM AND HUGH SEAGRIM ARE THE ONLY BROTHERS TO WIN THE VC AND GC BETWEEN THEM.

TASKER WATKINS VC

16 August 1944

Tasker Watkins (1918–2007). (IWM, HU 2034)

Tasker Watkins was born in Glamorgan, a week after the Armistice in 1918. He spent some of his childhood in Wales, before his family moved to Dagenham. He was working as an export agent when he enlisted in the Army at the outbreak of the Second World War.

He served in the ranks for 18 months before being commissioned in The Welch Regiment. In late June 1944, Watkins went to Normandy, joining the 1/5th Battalion as a lieutenant. By August, the Germans were fighting to hold their ground in the Falaise pocket. Watkins was commanding a company tasked with attacking objectives near the railway at Bafour, near Falaise, on the evening of 16 August.

As the company were making their way through booby-trapped cornfields towards the objective, they came under heavy fire. The company took heavy casualties, and the advance stopped. Watkins was the only officer left. He led from the front, and charged two machine gun posts in quick succession. He personally wounded or killed both the crews with his Sten gun.

As they reached their objective, the company stumbled across an anti-tank gun. Watkins turned his Sten gun on the gunner, but it jammed. The German did not immediately react, so Watkins threw the gun in his face, then shot him with his pistol.

By this time there were only around 30 men of the company left. Suddenly, 50 German infantry made a counter-attack. Watkins directed the

Watkins being invested with his Victoria Cross by George VI on 8 March 1945. On his return home in 1945, Dagenham made much of their first Victoria Cross recipient, putting on receptions in his honour, and presenting him with several collections. (Topfoto)

FIRST VICTORIA CROSS AWARDED TO A LIVING WELSHMAN IN THE SECOND WORLD WAR.

Rt Hon Sir Tasker Watkins as a Lord Justice of Appeal in 1992. He was appointed to the High Court Bench in 1971. In 1980, he became a Lord Justice of Appeal, and was made a member of the Privy Council. He was the first Senior Presiding Judge for England and Wales, 1983–91. (Topfoto)

fire of his men, before leading a bayonet charge which almost completely destroyed the Germans.

The light was fast fading. The rest of the battalion had withdrawn, but Watkins' company had not received the order as their radio was destroyed. Watkins considered holding the position, but his company was depleted, alone, and in danger of being surrounded. He decided to attempt to rejoin the battalion. As they passed through the treacherous cornfields once more, he was challenged by a nearby enemy post. He got his men to scatter, then went in alone, silencing the post with his Bren gun. Finally, he led his men back to battalion headquarters.

Watkins' actions, undertaken with total disregard for his own safety, had safeguarded the lives of many of his company. He was recommended for the Victoria Cross, confirmed in the command of his company, and promoted to captain. He was wounded in the Netherlands later that year, and evacuated back to Britain. In March 1945, Watkins received his Victoria Cross from the king.

After demobilisation, Watkins became a barrister and rose to become a Lord Justice of Appeal and deputy Lord Chief Justice. In later life he received many honours and decorations. Watkins was prominently involved with the Territorial Army Association in Wales, and president for Wales of the British Legion for many years. A great lover of rugby, Watkins was president of the Welsh Rugby Union. In 2006 Watkins was given the freedom of the city of Cardiff. He died in 2007. The funeral of this great Welshman was attended by hundreds. A large bronze statue of Watkins stands in Cardiff's Millennium Stadium.

'... it was just another day in the life of a soldier, I did what needed doing to help colleagues and friends, just as others looked out for me during the fighting that summer...'
Tasker Watkins

EUGENE ESMONDE VC

12 February 1942

Eugene 'Winkle' Esmonde (1909–42). (IWM, Courtesy of the Esmonde family)

Eugene Esmonde grew up in County Tipperary with his widowed mother and 12 siblings. He had studied to become a Catholic missionary, but in 1928 he took a five-year commission in the RAF, spending the last year with the Fleet Air Arm. He became a pilot with Imperial Airways, but left when the Fleet Air Arm offered him a commission in 1939. By now a very experienced pilot, Esmonde was given command of first a training command, and then 825 Squadron.

In May 1941, he led his squadron in an audacious attack on the *Bismarck*, scoring one hit. Esmonde received the Distinguished Service Order. The squadron was disbanded in late 1941, after many of their aircraft were lost when HMS *Ark Royal* sank. In early 1942, Lieutenant Commander Esmonde was rebuilding his squadron at RAF Manston on the south coast of England.

On 12 February, Esmonde was informed that two German battlecruisers and a cruiser escorted by around 30 ships, were entering the Dover Straits, making for the North German ports. Esmonde was ordered to attack them with torpedoes as soon as possible, before they reached the protection of the sandbanks north-east of Calais.

Eugene Esmonde's medal group. He was presented with his DSO the day before he was killed. (IWM, Courtesy of the Esmonde family)

He knew from the start that their mission was a forlorn hope. He would lead his half-strength squadron of six slow, antiquated Swordfish torpedo bombers, piloted by young, virtually untrained crews, in a daring attack on a fast-moving, well-protected group of ships. Their chances worsened when only one of the five Spitfire squadrons assigned to act as protection could get to them in time.

The fighter screen of Spitfires had difficulty staying with them because the Swordfish were so slow. Instead, Esmonde hoped to retain an element of surprise by approaching incredibly low at just 50 feet. Visibility was poor, and before the squadron got anywhere close to the cruisers, they were attacked by large numbers of German fighters. The lower port wing

EUGENE ESMONDE'S GREAT-UNCLE, THOMAS ESMONDE, RECEIVED A VICTORIA CROSS FOR HIS BRAVERY AT SEBASTAPOL IN 1855.

For his calmness against impossible odds, and for continuing his gallant leadership even when his own plane had been seriously damaged, Esmonde was posthumously awarded the Victoria Cross. The other 17 men were also decorated.

'The last that was seen of this gallant band who were astern of the leading flight is that they were flying steadily towards the battle-cruiser. Their aircraft were shattered. Undeterred by the inferno of fire, they carried out their orders, which were to attack the target. Not one came back. Theirs was courage which is beyond praise.'
London Gazette

Esmonde leading his Swordfish squadron against the battlecruisers *Scharnhorst* and *Gneisenau*, and the cruiser *Prinz Eugen*. Despite their efforts, and subsequent attempts, all three ships escaped. (The National Archives)

of Esmonde's bi-plane was shattered, but he managed to regain control, and flew on steadily towards the target. Contact had been lost with the fighter screen, but this did not deter Esmonde. He led his aircraft over the German destroyer screen. Almost immediately, his aircraft was shot down by an enemy fighter, and he and his two crew crashed into the Channel. However, his example had so inspired his squadron that they continued, and at least one torpedo hit the enemy ships. None of the six aircraft returned, and only a few survivors were picked up from the Channel.

MANLEY ANGELL JAMES VC

21 March 1918

Manley Angell James (1896–1975). James is a very rare example of an officer being decorated for gallantry in both world wars. (IWM, VC 631)

Manley James was born in Hampshire, and after school, joined the Gloucestershire Regiment in 1915. In the summer of 1916, he was severely wounded on the Somme. He returned to France later that year as a staff officer. But he was determined to return to the action, and by early 1917 he was back on the front line with his regiment. That year he was wounded again, mentioned in dispatches, and received the Military Cross. James was a courageous leader and a much-loved officer, held in high esteem by his men.

On 21 March 1918, the German spring offensive was launched, and the 8th Battalion, Gloucestershire Regiment at Vélu Wood, was in the thick of the determined German assault.

As the attack began, James led A Company forward against the Germans and captured 27 prisoners and two machine guns. He was wounded, but refused to leave his company. The following day there were three German attacks on their position but the Glosters under James' determined leadership held their line. On 23 March, the enemy finally broke through on the right, but James refused to retreat. A senior officer ordered him to hold his position to the last. He made a heroic last stand, inflicting heavy losses, and giving the battalion time to withdraw in good order. James led his company forward in a counter-attack, and was wounded yet again. Finally their position collapsed and James told his men to run. He was last seen working a machine gun alone, sporting a third wound.

His selfless actions at Vélu Wood enabled the Brigade to be withdrawn successfully and survive to fight another day. If his company had not held the enemy back, the entire battalion might have been completely cut off. But there was a high price to pay: 75 per cent of his company were lost in the fighting. Eyewitnesses stated that they had seen James killed, but he had actually been taken prisoner. After treatment for his wounds, he spent the remaining months of the war in a prisoner-of-war camp. It wasn't until late May that his family discovered he was still alive, and his Victoria Cross was announced the following month.

James was repatriated after the Armistice and managed, after some effort, to get a regular commission as a Lieutenant in December 1920. By 1942, he was a brigadier. For his leadership of the 128th Infantry Brigade in Algeria he received the Distinguished Service Order. His citation said that he was 'personally as brave as a lion'. After North Africa he served in Italy, then trained troops for D-Day. After the Second World War he commanded the RAF's troops in Germany during the Occupation for three years, before becoming Director of Ground Defence at the Air Ministry. He finally retired in 1951, and was made an MBE seven years later.

'Captain James said to us few left we are surrounded boys every man for himself he then got on the fire step and started firing at the advancing enemy telling us to run if we could possibly get away'
Survivor of A Co

Manley James' medal group. (Courtesy of the Lord Ashcroft Collection)

SKILL

'the highest courage, tactical skill and coolness'

Wisdom, sound judgement and technical knowledge are the hallmarks of Skill.
It is about using resources to greatest effect, usually under intense pressure. For many
involved in bomb disposal, for example, while a single wrong move might start the clock
ticking, the puzzle still has to be solved, the game won. Perseverance is everything.

THOMAS HOPPER ALDERSON GC

1940

Thomas Alderson (1903–65) after his investiture. A ward at Bridlington Hospital is named after him, as is a road in the town. (IWM, HU 65861, by permission of Mrs Pamela Wilson)

Thomas Alderson's medal group. He received the RSPCA Silver Medal for heroism for rescuing two horses trapped in a bombed stable. (IWM, by kind permission of Mrs Pamela Wilson)

Born in Sunderland in 1903, Thomas Alderson was the fifth of six children. Leaving school at 15, he started as an office boy in the local ironworks, but soon became a draughtsman then completed a five-year engineering apprenticeship. He joined the Merchant Navy in 1925, eventually becoming First Engineer. After nine years in the Merchant Navy, he settled in Bridlington with his family. He worked for local authorities, becoming Works Supervisor with Bridlington Corporation. In 1938, he attended Air Raid Precaution (ARP) training, which was then actively recruiting volunteers for local ARP organizations, in preparation for the expected air attacks on Britain in the event of war.

When the Second World War broke out, Alderson led the Rescue and Demolition Squads, responsible for rescuing people from bomb-damaged buildings. The port of Bridlington was bombed by the Luftwaffe early in the war, and residential areas nearby were also affected. On at least three occasions in August 1940, Alderson rescued trapped civilians from the dangerous ruins of buildings. On 15 August, he tunnelled into a demolished pair of semi-detached houses to rescue a woman. The second rescue was on 20 August, and carried out when two five-storey buildings collapsed, trapping 11 people in cellars. Alderson admitted that this one was probably the worst incident. Six of the survivors were buried in debris as the cellar they had sheltered in had given way. To get to them, Alderson tunnelled around 14 feet under the unsafe wreckage of the houses, working for four hours in very cramped conditions, with only hand torches to provide light. Enemy aircraft were still flying overhead, and fractured water pipes and gas pipes made the work even more dangerous. Though badly bruised himself, he managed to help all those trapped reach safety without any further injuries.

On the third occasion, 23 August, five people were trapped in a cellar below several collapsed four-storey buildings. Constantly in danger from an unstable wall swaying above where the rescue was happening, Alderson led the rescue team in digging a tunnel from the pavement, through the foundations, into the cellar. He then personally tunnelled under the wreckage into the cellar, which was in danger of further collapse, managing to rescue two people alive from underneath a large refrigerator. He continued to work even though enemy aircraft were heard overhead and air raid warnings were given.

For his courage and devotion to duty, he became the first person to receive the George Cross from the king, gazetted on 30 September, and presented on 20 May 1941.

Alderson carried on his rescue work. After the war, he joined the East Riding council. He then joined the new Civil Defence Corps, ready to protect the population from nuclear warfare. He died of lung cancer in 1965.

'I feel very honoured to have been awarded the George Cross, but don't forget that all the men of the Bridlington rescue parties were there too.'
Thomas Alderson on the radio after the presentation

THOMAS ALDERSON WAS THE FIRST PERSON TO BE AWARDED THE GEORGE CROSS.

LLOYD ALLAN TRIGG VC

11 August 1943

Lloyd Trigg (1914–43). His initial military service was with the Army, serving in a territorial unit until 1934. (Topfoto)

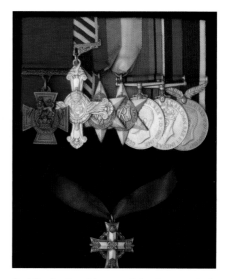

Lloyd Allan Trigg's medal group, including the New Zealand Memorial Cross awarded after his death. (Courtesy of the Lord Ashcroft Collection)

Lloyd Trigg was born in North Auckland, New Zealand and enlisted in the Royal New Zealand Air Force in 1941. After training and commissioning, he was posted to 200 Squadron, Royal Air Force in 1942. Flying Hudson aircraft from a base in West Africa, Trigg undertook reconnaissance, convoy escort and anti-submarine patrols over the Atlantic.

In March 1943, he was awarded the Distinguished Flying Cross for his actions against German U-boats. These missions were extremely dangerous. German U-boat tactics had evolved throughout the war and they now patrolled the high seas in formidable groups or 'wolfpacks', carrying improved anti-aircraft defences. They did not immediately dive when aircraft appeared, instead staying on the surface to battle it out. For airmen and submariners, the consequences of these deadly duels were often dire, few who ended up in the freezing waters of the north Atlantic had any chance of survival.

In mid-1943 Trigg undertook conversion training for Liberator bombers in the Bahamas, arriving back in West Africa in July 1943. By this time he was a highly experienced and skilled pilot who had completed 46 sorties.

On 11 August 1943 Trigg undertook his first operational sortie in a Liberator. He took off from Yundum, with a crew of six. It was a routine patrol, covering the areas where U-boats were most likely to be operating. After eight hours, they spotted a U-boat on the surface, fitted with the latest anti-aircraft guns.

Trigg prepared to attack. On the first two passes over the U-boat, the Liberator took many hits, and after the second run, the tail was on fire. Trigg could have broken off the engagement at this point and made a forced landing in the Atlantic, as there was no possibility of making it back to base. His other option was to make his final attack on the U-boat, but this would drastically reduce his crew's chances of survival.

Trigg maintained course. Flying at less than 50 feet, with anti-aircraft fire entering the open bomb doors, he dropped his depth charges. A shell from the U-boat hit the Liberator squarely. The aircraft dived into the sea, and sank in a matter of seconds.

The U-boat was severely damaged, and sank within 20 minutes. Seven of the survivors managed to reach the Liberator's rubber dinghy, which was floating loose. The dinghy was sighted by an RAF aircraft, and then eventually picked up by HMS *Clarkia*, at which point it was realised that the men in it were not the crew of the Liberator, as had been assumed. The Germans told their rescuers about the daring attack of the Liberator, and on the basis of this testimony, Trigg was awarded a posthumous Victoria Cross. This is the only instance where a Victoria Cross has been awarded on the testimony of the enemy.

LLOYD TRIGG WAS THE FIRST AIRMAN TO BE AWARDED THE VICTORIA CROSS FOR ACTIONS AGAINST A U-BOAT.

Edward Kinder Bradbury VC
George Thomas Dorrell VC
David Nelson VC

1 September 1914

The action of L Battery at Néry was an iconic action during the retreat from Mons in 1914. The battery had landed in France on 16 August. They saw action at Audrignies on 24 August, Le Cateau on 26 August, and by 31 August, they had retreated behind the Aisne. It must have been a relief to the exhausted men when they were ordered to bivouack near Néry, a village about 30 miles north-east of Paris.

The men of L Battery were up at 2.30am, and by 4.30am were ready to move out, but due to fog, they were put on standby, ready to move at 15 minutes' notice. While waiting they watered the horses and prepared breakfast.

Unknown to the British, the German 4th Cavalry Division had also spent the night in the area, only 2 miles away. A British patrol had just discovered the Germans when the fog lifted shortly after 5am, but the Germans had found them first, and the enemy guns opened fire with devastating effect. L Battery were closest to the enemy, and the result was terrible. Men and horses were mown down where they stood, with horses breaking loose and stampeding.

Captain Bradbury had been standing a little way away from the battery with some other officers prior to the German attack. As the firing began, Bradbury shouted 'Come on! Who's for the guns?' and ran back into the chaos, where the panicking horses were doing further damage to the guns.

Only three of the six 13-pounders could be brought into action against the 12 German guns. Sergeant Nelson and Captain Bradbury got No.6 gun

Left: Edward Bradbury (1881–1914). Bradbury was buried in the village communal cemetery along with others from the battery. (IWM, VC 115)
Middle: George Dorrell (1880–1971). He joined the Army at the age of 15 giving his age as 19. He was made MBE in later life. (IWM, Q 79792)
Right: David Nelson (1886–1918). After the action, Nelson was taken to a temporary field hospital. The next day, the hospital was taken by the Germans. Still in considerable pain, Nelson escaped in his slippers, reaching French forces to tell them what had happened. (IWM, Q 80586)

into action with assistance from Gunner Darbyshire, Driver Osborne and others. The other two guns were soon disabled, and the survivors of their crews joined No.6 gun. Darbyshire and Osborne brought ammunition from the wagon 20 yards away while Lieutenant Mundy acted as observer, Bradbury as layer, and Nelson as range-setter. Despite the fire of all the German guns being concentrated on No.6 gun, it remained untouched, and it was exacting its own deadly punishment on the German guns, just 800 yards away.

At 6.30am, Mundy and Nelson were badly wounded. Bradbury and Nelson continued to fire the gun, but the rate of fire was dropping. At 7.15, Battery Sergeant Major Dorrell, an experienced and highly trained gunner, reached the gun, and took over laying. Ammunition was low, and Bradbury went to get more, but was mortally wounded when a shell severed his leg. He continued to help, until another shell took off his other leg. He reportedly asked the doctor for large quantities of morphia, so that the men would not have to hear him scream. Now only Dorrell and Nelson remained, with Nelson suffering from a serious chest wound. Eventually they ran out of ammunition but not until they had knocked out the guns

No.6 gun in action at Néry. The casualties taken by the Battery at Néry were devastating: 45 officers and men from 170, and 150 of the 228 horses. (Bridgeman)

ranged against them. They fired the last two rounds at around 7.30am, just as reinforcements arrived to drive away the Germans, capturing eight guns and taking prisoners.

The action at Néry went down in regimental history as 'Dorrell's duel'. Dorrell, Nelson and Bradbury all received the Victoria Cross for this historic stand. Osborne and Darbyshire were both awarded the Medaille Militaire. Dorrell and Nelson were commissioned following the action. Nelson rose to the rank of major, but was killed at Lillers in 1918. Dorrell had brought what was left of the battery home in 1914, later returning to France as a battery commander. He left the Army in 1921, and served with the Home Guard during the Second World War. He died in 1971 aged 90, and was given a regimental funeral.

The battery was awarded the honorific title 'L (Néry) Battery', the Royal Horse Artillery in recognition of the action. To this day every year on 1 September the Battery celebrates Néry day. For years, this celebration was complete with a competitive re-enaction, with gun crews competing to be the first to dress, assemble their guns, manhandle them through an obstacle course and fire a blank round.

'So terrific was the hail of shrapnel that I was bespattered with blood from men and horses...'
David Nelson

After the battle, No.6 gun was salvaged. It was kept as a memento in its damaged condition and has been on display at the IWM since around 1920. (IWM, ORD 102)

WILLIAM LEEFE ROBINSON VC

2/3 September 1916

In 1914 William Leefe Robinson entered the Royal Military College, Sandhurst and was commissioned into the Worcestershire Regiment. He was posted to Cornwall but, eager to see action, he transferred to the Royal Flying Corps in France. He served as an observer for two months until he was wounded. Upon recovery, Robinson trained as a pilot and was posted to several home defence squadrons around London. Upon re-organisation of these squadrons into 39 (Home Defence) Squadron, Lieutenant Robinson took command of B Flight, based at Suttons Farm, on the eastern outskirts of London.

Zeppelin raids on London had started in May 1915. In late April 1916 Robinson had his first encounter with a German air-ship. Despite his best efforts, he made no impact on the huge target, then lost it in the darkness. Frustrated, he vowed that next time he met one, he would take it down. There were no more raids for the next few months, but 2 September saw the largest raid yet, of 16 German air-ships.

B Flight was on readiness, and when the War Office rang with orders to intercept the raiders, Robinson took off into the damp and foggy night. He had almost finished patrolling his area and was giving up hope of making contact, when he saw an airship, the *LZ98*, which had bombed Gravesend. Robinson was high above the air-ship, and was gaining on it, when it vanished

William Leefe Robinson's medal group. (Courtesy of the Lord Ashcroft Collection)

into cloud. After 15 minutes of vain searching, Robinson gave up and made for base. As he did so, he saw *SL11* held in searchlights to the north.

He decided to attack, even though anti-aircraft defences were targeting the air-ship with heavy fire, which would also endanger his own aircraft. Reaching the air-ship, he dived down below it and attacked, emptying an entire drum of Lewis gun bullets into the huge air-ship. Despite this the air-ship seemed undamaged. Robinson changed the drum on his gun and repeated his attack, emptying the bullets into the side of the air-ship.

William Leefe Robinson (1895–1918). He was born in India and lived there with his family until he was sent to England to attend school. (IWM, Q 66470)

FIRST VICTORIA CROSS WON FOR ACTION IN THE UNITED KINGDOM.

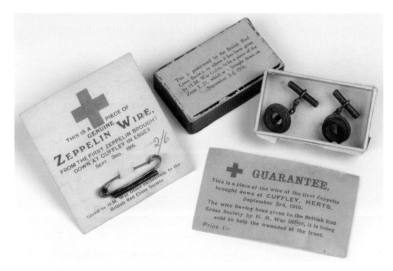

Fragments of wreckage from the air-ship were sold by the British Red Cross Society to raise money for the wounded at the front. (IWM, EPH 9441–9443)

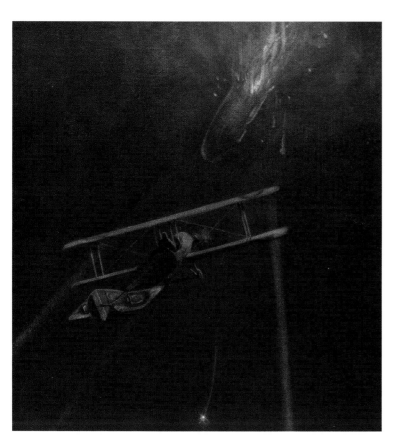

An illustration of Robinson bringing down *SL11*, from *Deeds that Thrill the Empire*. There is a memorial to Robinson at Cuffley, Hertfordshire, where the air-ship crashed. (Bridgeman)

Newspaper hoarding after the action. Robinson became a celebrity within days of his action, recognised and congratulated everywhere he went. He also received over £4,000 in prize money from grateful donors. (IWM, LI 2009 99 135 2, Courtesy of the Lord Ashcroft Collection)

The blazing airship lit up the sky for 60 miles before exploding, and finally crashed in Hertfordshire. *SL11* was the first air-ship to be brought down over England, and thousands of people flocked into the streets to watch. It was probably the greatest sensation of the war, and a huge morale-booster to the population who had watched Zeppelins raid London and the east coast for many months with apparent impunity.

Robinson was recommended for a Victoria Cross, which was gazetted three days after his action. He received his decoration from the king at Windsor Castle on 9 September, the same day that the 16 crew of the air-ship were buried.

After a rest from flying on active service, Robinson was posted as a Flight Commander to 48 Squadron. They went to France in March 1917. On 5 April, Robinson led six Bristol fighters on their first patrol over the front line. The patrol came up against five German fighters led by Freiherr, Manfred von Richthofen. Robinson was forced to land behind German lines and spent the rest of the war as a prisoner-of-war.

He escaped twice, but was recaptured, and was given several spells in solitary confinement, before being transferred to a camp renowned for harsh treatment of prisoners. He returned to England in mid-December 1918, his health broken. That Christmas he caught influenza and died on 31 December. He was buried a few days later with full military honours.

The air-ship seemed oblivious to the attack, and did not return fire. Robinson reloaded once more, and got in very close underneath and behind the ship, concentrating his fire on the same spot. Initially it seemed to have as little effect as his previous attacks, but a few seconds later, the entire air-ship was on fire. Robinson was forced to take quick evasive action as the burning *SL11* plunged towards the ground. Robinson watched it fall, then returned to Suttons Farm, landing with an almost empty fuel tank having been in the air for three and a half hours.

RODERICK ALISTAIR BROOK LEAROYD VC

12/13 August 1940

Roderick Learoyd (1913–96) painted in 1940. A lifelong car enthusiast, Learoyd attended Chelsea College of Aeronautical and Automobile Engineering and after the war worked for the British Motor Corporation. He was known in the RAF as 'Babe'. (IWM, LD 412)

Roderick Learoyd joined the RAF on a short service commission in 1936. Following training, he was posted to 49 Squadron. By March 1940, Learoyd had already flown over 20 wartime operations and was an acting Flight Lieutenant.

On 12 August, he led 11 Hampden bombers in an attack on the old aqueduct carrying the Dortmund-Ems Canal over the Ems River near Münster. The route that incoming enemy bombers would be forced to take was predictable, so the Germans had prepared their defences accordingly. The slow and poorly defended Hampdens would face hundreds of anti-aircraft guns and scores of searchlights. Learoyd had previously attacked the canal himself, so he was well aware of the risks they would face.

Eight of the force safely reached the target. Five bombers from 49 Squadron were allocated the bombing of the aqueduct itself, while the

Roderick Learoyd's medal group. Learoyd's crew were all decorated for the raid. (Courtesy of the Lord Ashcroft Collection)

Learoyd's raid over the Dortmund-Ems canal. The canal was a vital route for the transport of raw materials and military support to the German Army. The bombs destroyed the aqueduct, and put the canal out of action for ten days. (Mary Evans)

other three made diversionary attacks. The bombs they carried had a time delay of ten minutes. The bombers would approach and drop their bombs at two-minute intervals. Timing was of the utmost importance, as a delay could mean that the last bomber, Learoyd's, would be directly above when the first bomb detonated. Learoyd circled as the other bombers made their runs. Two went down in flames, and the remaining two were damaged. The defences were now at full alert, and the anti-aircraft fire intensified as Learoyd got closer to the aqueduct. Dropping down to 150ft, his Hampden was soon damaged by the flak. Larger and larger pieces of his aircraft fell away as he approached the target. The searchlights completely blinded Learoyd, and he had to rely on his instruments, and guidance from his navigator. But he carried on regardless, and dropped his bomb. The Hampden was low enough that his wireless officer actually saw it land on the aqueduct.

Learoyd's Hampden was in bad shape, with landing gear and flaps and undercarriage indicators all now out of action. He managed to coax his aircraft back to England, but the damage to the bomber meant he could not land in the dark. He had to fly around for almost three more hours until it was light enough to bring the aircraft down in an emergency landing. He was awarded the Victoria Cross for the courage and skill he had displayed on the raid.

Learoyd continued to fly operationally, becoming a wing commander, and later taking command of 44 Squadron. A shy, quiet man, he rarely spoke about his wartime exploits. In later life he suffered from diabetes, which affected his sight, but he remained an active member of the Victoria Cross and George Cross Association until his death.

EVERARD ALOYSIUS LISLE PHILLIPPS VC

30 May–18 September 1857

Everard Aloysius Lisle Phillipps (1835–57). Born and raised in Leicestershire, he was a keen sportsman. (Courtesy of the Royal Green Jackets Museum)

Everard Lisle Phillipps was 19 when he was commissioned as an Ensign in the 11th Bengal Native Infantry, Bengal Army in 1854. He was present at the very beginning of the Indian Mutiny in Meerut on 10 May 1857, and was actually standing beside Colonel John Finnis when Finnis was shot by a mutinous sepoy as he prepared to deliver an address to persuade the Army to remain loyal. Phillipps then allegedly had to read out the queen's proclamation against the insurgents. His horse was shot from under him when he began to read it, and he fell to the ground, wounded. He then jumped up, read through the whole proclamation again before rapidly taking cover. Phillipps managed to escape Meerut, and over the next few months he was at the forefront of several battles, many attached to the 60th Rifles, being wounded several times in the process.

In the assault on Delhi on 14 September, Phillipps, leading some riflemen, was among the first to mount the walls of the city. He led the capture of the Water Bastion, and turned the guns of the bastion on the mutineers within the city. For his gallantry in this action, Phillipps was awarded a permanent commission in the 60th Rifles.

He was then involved in the savage fighting through the streets of Delhi. But on 18 September, he was finally shot and killed at Bank House while supervising the building of defences. He was buried in Delhi the same day.

In 1859, his exploits during the Indian Mutiny were noted in the *London Gazette*, with the explanation that he would have been recommended for the Victoria Cross had he not been killed. At that time, the Victoria Cross was not awarded posthumously. Over the next decades, Phillipps' family made several attempts to obtain the Victoria Cross they felt was rightfully his. It was not until 1907 that the six men who had been recorded in the *Gazette* as likely to receive the Victoria Cross, had they survived, were finally granted it posthumously. A Victoria Cross for Phillipps was sent to his next of kin, his brother. However, when it came up for auction in 1998, it became apparent that both the medal and the presentation box were different to the standard Victoria Cross. It was withdrawn from sale while enquiries were made into whether it was actually a real VC, or just a fake. Research suggested that it was in fact an 'unofficial' medal, given by Queen Victoria to Phillipps' mother sometime in the 1870s.

The Memorandum Victoria Cross given to Phillipps' family by Queen Victoria, as was the procedure before posthumous VCs. (Courtesy of the Lord Ashcroft Collection)

CHRISTOPHER AUGUSTUS COX VC

13–17 March 1917

Christopher Cox (1889–1959). He lived in Kings Langley from birth until death, apart from the war years. He died in 1959, having never fully recovered from falling from a roof a few years previously. (The Kings Langley Local History & Museum Society)

In September 1914, Christopher Cox left his small village in Hertfordshire to enlist in the 7th Battalion, Bedfordshire Regiment. The following July, his regiment left for France.

A tall, powerful man, Cox volunteered to be a stretcher-bearer. He spent the next two years on the Western Front, treating men on the battlefield and carrying them to safety. He was wounded in the leg on the first day of the Somme in 1916, but after two months of treatment he was back with his battalion for the battle for Thiepval in the September of that year.

In March 1917, his battalion fought a bloody battle near Achiet-le-Grand as the Germans fell back on the Hindenburg Line. For five days they advanced across two miles of open ground, taking heavy casualties from the artillery and machine gun fire of the German rearguard.

Throughout the advance, Cox put himself in the utmost danger, as he went out onto open ground under heavy fire, time after time to treat and rescue wounded soldiers. On the first day, Cox single-handedly treated and rescued four men. Having helped all the wounded of his company, he went back out and helped bring in other wounded soldiers. After bringing in wounded machine gunners, he even made further trips into the battle to collect their ammunition. Eyewitnesses stated that he seemed to simply ignore the bullets flying all around him.

The shrapnel that wounded Cox in 1917. He had to undergo an operation to remove the bullets, before being sent back to Blighty. (The Kings Langley Local History & Museum Society)

Over the next few days he made further similar rescues. On the 16th and 17th he went to the very front of the attack to bring in wounded men. He was so far forward that he was able to stop and mark the gaps in the barbed wire for the soldiers rushing up to reinforce the attack, before carrying wounded men back through the wire to the dressing stations. He continued his work even when the soldiers were digging in on each day, returning to his company late in the evening, on the verge of total exhaustion.

Over several days, his efforts saved the lives of many of his comrades, and the men of his company all gave evidence of his sterling efforts. On the basis of their evidence, he was recommended for the Victoria Cross. A few weeks later, he was seriously wounded in the foot at Cherisy and invalided back to England. He was awarded his Victoria Cross by George V in July 1917 at Buckingham Palace.

After the war, Cox returned to his home village of Kings Langley. A quiet unassuming man, he worked in the Ovaltine factory for many years, and he and his wife had eight children. During the Second World War he served in the Home Guard, showing his courage once more when he entered a bombed-out pub to search for survivors.

'I was only doing what any British soldier would have done.'
Christopher Augustus Cox VC

'In spite of the heavy bombardment he never hesitated to take back a second case having just returned from taking one.'
2nd Lieutenant S. R. Chapman

ROBERT JOHN DAVIES GC

12 September 1940

Robert Davies (1900–75). He joined the Canadian Army during the First World War. (IWM, HU 7995)

The St Paul's bomb was the biggest bomb yet dropped on London, and the whole area had to be cordoned off until Davies and his men had removed it. St Paul's became an beacon of hope to the population of London during the Blitz, its destruction would have been a huge blow to public morale. (IWM, HU 3046)

Born in Cornwall, Robert Davies emigrated to Canada as a young man, and also spent time living and working in America and East Africa. By 1940, Davies was back in England, where he joined the Royal Engineers and trained in bomb disposal.

The night of 12 September 1940 saw heavy bombing over London. Lieutenant Davies was the officer of a section of No.5 Bomb Disposal Company, Royal Engineers, who were sent to the area around St Paul's Cathedral to deal with unexploded bombs there.

Davies and his men found a one-ton bomb which had hit the pavement at the south-west corner of the cathedral. The bomb had penetrated the method for dealing with it had not yet been developed so the advice was to perform a controlled explosion. But this bomb was so close to the cathedral that an explosion would have caused a huge amount of damage to this national monument. The decision was made to try and extract it complete.

Initially work was slow, as a gas main had been severed, but when the fire had been put out, and the gas turned off, the digging could begin. Electrical cables had also been severed, adding extra danger to the men's task. As they dug, the bomb slipped around another 12 feet before it was finally secured.

The bomb was pulled from the ground by two lorries linked in tandem, and quickly loaded onto a lorry. To protect his men, Davies drove the lorry himself out to Hackney Marshes where he finally detonated the bomb. The detonation made a crater 100 feet wide.

For his bravery despite the obvious danger, Robert Davies became the first serviceman to be awarded the new George Cross, instituted by King George VI that month. Sapper George Wylie was also awarded the George Cross, and other members of the team were awarded British Empire Medals. Although among the first to be gazetted for the George Cross, Davies wasn't presented with his medal until February 1942, due to his operational deployment to the Middle East. That same year Davies was court-martialled for charges relating to fraud and dishonesty while commanding a bomb disposal unit in London. He was said to have used soldiers to build air raid shelters for friends using stolen government supplies. He was found guilty on several charges and dismissed from the Army. After the war, Davies emigrated to Australia with his family, where he lived until his death. He sold his George Cross in 1970.

Bomb damage outside of St Paul's. (London Metropolitan Archives)

ground, ending up around 15 feet underground, almost beneath the clock tower. On examination, the bomb was found to have an anti-withdrawal device. This device had only been seen a few times before, and a successful

'The explosion caused a 100ft crater and windows rattled and plaster loosen in houses for many miles around.'
Robert Davies GC

DAVID SAMUEL ANTHONY LORD VC

19 September 1944

David Lord was born in Ireland in 1913 where his father was serving with the British Army. The family spent some time in India, before settling in Wrexham. He became a journalist and writer, but a fascination with flying led to him enlist in the RAF in 1936 for six years' service. He trained as a pilot and was posted to India, where he was a supply pilot on the North-West Frontier. In 1941 he flew evacuation flights out of Iraq. He then flew supply missions to the Chindits in Japanese-occupied Burma, dangerous missions undertaken over enemy territory without fighter escort. He was commissioned in 1942 and the following year he received the Distinguished Flying Cross for his large number of sorties. By the time he returned to England, in 1944, he was a highly experienced pilot. He was posted to 271 Squadron, where he was trained to tow gliders, drop airborne troops and supplies. He took part in the D-Day operations, and then in September 1944, Operation *Market Garden*.

On 19 September, Flight Lieutenant Lord was pilot and captain of Dakota KG374, dropping supplies to the airborne troops at Arnhem. Because the troops were surrounded by the Germans, the drops had to be incredibly accurate otherwise the supplies might fall into enemy hands. To ensure accuracy, the aircraft had to fly in at 900 feet, dangerously exposing it to enemy fire. As Lord got close to the drop zone, the starboard wing of his Dakota

David Lord's medal group. (Courtesy of the Lord Ashcroft Collection)

David Lord (1913–44). Lord is buried in the Oosterbeek Military cemetery in Arnhem, beside his crew. There are several memorials to Lord, including a VC-10 of No.10 Sqn named *David Lord VC.* (IWM, HU 1233)

was hit twice by anti-aircraft fire, setting the engine ablaze. Lord could have abandoned the mission, but as his crew were uninjured and they were only three minutes away from the drop zone, he chose to continue.

As they came in for the final approach, the starboard engine was burning furiously, and the aircraft was singled out for anti-aircraft fire. Despite this, Lord skilfully kept the aircraft straight and level while the supplies were dropped. After the run, two containers of supplies still remained. Though the wing could collapse at any moment, Lord circled, rejoined the stream of aircraft and made a second run to drop the supplies, again assaulted by heavy fire. It is said that his second run was anxiously watched by all the Allied troops on the ground hoping to see the crew jump before it was too late.

These manoeuvres had taken eight minutes. The Dakota was now down to 500ft. Lord ordered his crew to abandon the aircraft. He made no attempt to leave it himself, staying at the controls to keep the aircraft steady as the others prepared to jump. Seconds later, the wing collapsed, the engine exploded and the Dakota fell in flames. Only the navigator survived. Blown out of the aircraft by the explosion, he managed to join the troops on the ground, and was eventually taken prisoner. On his release in 1945, he reported Lord's action, and the pilot's skilful use of his aircraft and his grim determination to re-supply the beleaguered troops on the ground was recognised with the posthumous award of a Victoria Cross.

LORD IS THE ONLY RECIPIENT OF THE VICTORIA CROSS FROM THE RAF'S TRANSPORT COMMAND.

SACRIFICE

'deliberately gave his life for his comrade'

In what is apparently the simplest quality of bravery, Sacrifice epitomises selfless responsibility.
Noble, strong, dependable, life is offered up to protect, save or comfort others. It is not always lost,
but it is always freely given. Death is expected, even if sometimes it does not arrive.
With strong religious overtones, Sacrifice is clear and straight, like the clean lines of a cross.

JOHN ALAN QUINTON GC
13 August 1951

John Alan Quinton (1921–51). Among the memorials to this extraordinary man was the Quinton Trophy which until 1993 was awarded annually at RAF Halton to the highest achieving ATC cadet. (IWM, HU 3161)

John Quinton was born in 1921 in London. After school he joined an engineering company as an apprentice. He could have remained there as an exempt employee throughout the Second World War, but in 1941 he joined the RAF as a navigator. He flew in night-fighters, and his work was consistently rated as exceptional. In 1944 he was awarded the Distinguished Flying Cross, and unusually for a navigator, he became a flight commander.

After the war he returned to his job, then later moved to a car accessory company. He married, and had a son, Roger. In 1951 he re-joined the RAF serving with 228 Operational Conversion Unit. He had to start again as a Flight Lieutenant, rather than at his old rank of Squadron Leader.

In August 1951, Quinton was about to finish his refresher course when the Wellington he was training in collided with a two-seater Miles Martinet that was acting as 'target' for the trainee navigators over Yorkshire. He was in the rear compartment of the aircraft with Derek Coates, a 16-year-old Air Training Corps cadet on his first flight. The collision caused the Wellington to break up, and as it began to plunge to earth Quinton grabbed the only parachute within reach and clipped it onto the terrified air cadet. He pointed to the rip-cord and a gaping hole in the aircraft, indicating that the boy should jump. At that moment another part of the aircraft was ripped away and the cadet was flung out of the aircraft. He managed to open his parachute and land safely. Derek Coates was the only survivor of the crash; the other eight people in the two aircraft all perished. When he explained how he had survived, he was asked to name the man who had saved his life. Unable to do so, he was shown photographs of the crew, and he immediately picked out John Quinton.

As his citation described, Quinton 'acted with superhuman speed, displaying the most commendable courage and self-sacrifice as he well knew that in giving up the only parachute within reach he was forfeiting any chance of saving his own life'.

Following Coates' account, Quinton was recommended for a posthumous George Cross. His widow received his medal from Elizabeth II at the first investiture of her reign in February 1952.

John Quinton's medal group. He had served with distinction throughout the Second World War before the posthumous award of his George Cross in 1951. (IWM, lent by the Quinton family)

BASIL JOHN DOUGLAS GUY VC

13 July 1900

Basil Guy (1882–1956), who joined the cadet training ship HMS *Britannia* immediately after finishing school before passing out to HMS *Barfleur* in 1898. He served during the Boxer Rebellion and both World Wars and received the DSO during the First World War. (IWM, Q 79770)

The Boxer rebellion of 1900 saw 140,000 'Boxers' attack foreign embassies in Beijing, and missions throughout the country in response to imperialist expansion and missionary evangelism. In July 1900, the Boxers took control of the city of Tientsin. Basil Guy, the son of a vicar from County Durham, was an 18-year-old midshipman serving onshore alongside other sailors, marines and officers from HMS *Barfleur* as part of a relief force. On 13 July, during the battle for Tientsin, the force had to cross about 150 yards of open area. While they were doing so, they came under heavy fire, which caused several casualties. Able Seaman McCarthy was shot and fell around 50 yards from safety. Guy stayed with him and tried to carry him to safety, but was unable to do so. The rest of the company were now under cover, so the heavy fire from the city walls was concentrated on McCarthy and Guy, and the ground around them was ploughed up by bullets. Guy bound McCarthy's wound with his handkerchief, then ran to get help.

The stretchers arrived to aid the wounded of the relief force just as Guy got to cover. Guy went back to McCarthy with a carrying party, and helped bring him in. Sadly the sailor was shot again while he lay on the stretcher, and he died before reaching safety.

For his brave actions taken with no regard for his own safety, Guy was recommended for the Victoria Cross by a major of the Marines who had helped bring the wounded seaman in. It was gazetted in November 1900. He was said to have been completely surprised when, some months later, he happened to hear his name read out by a signalman taking in a signal giving names for promotions and decorations. He had no idea that he had done anything special, or that it had even been recommended or mentioned.

He was presented with his Victoria Cross in March 1902 by Edward VII. The following year he was promoted to Lieutenant for his service in China.

During the First World War he was awarded the DSO for his command of the Q-ship *Wonganella* during an encounter with a U-boat. He was promoted to Commander in 1918, and retired from the Navy in 1923. He married in 1917, and had two daughters. Following his retirement, he became a poultry farmer but with the outbreak of war once again in 1939 he was recalled and served for the duration of the conflict.

Basil Guy's sword. (IWM, LI 2009 999 62 31, Courtesy of the Lord Ashcroft Collection)

Matthew Croucher GC

Matt Croucher after receiving his George Cross. He has written a book about his experiences, *Bulletproof*, and uses his status as a holder of the George Cross to help charities such as Help for Heroes. (National Pictures/Topfoto)

Matt Croucher grew up in Birmingham and joined the Royal Marines at the age of 16. After successfully completing their legendary training course, he joined 40 Commando but initially he could not serve overseas as he was only 17. He served two tours in Iraq and was one of the first 200 Allied soldiers to invade the country in 2003. His commando service saw him escape death on many occasions, and during his second tour of duty he was back in action a week after a roadside bomb attack left him with a fractured skull. After his two tours, he became a reservist, and returned to Iraq as a private security contractor. He was called back from the reserve in late 2007, and went to Afghanistan once again as a Royal Marine with 40 Commando.

In November 2007, Croucher helped save the life of a seriously wounded comrade during a fire-fight, applying first aid until the man could be extracted. Later that month, while providing security for a night air drop, he was injured, and evacuated to the UK with a suspected broken leg. Determined to return to theatre, he resumed his duties with Commando Reconnaissance Force within weeks.

On 9 February 2008, Lance-Corporal Croucher was part of a four-man team that entered a compound, thought to be occupied, to investigate whether it was a bomb-making factory.

Moving very cautiously in the dark, they found proof of bomb-making, at which point the team commander decided they should return to where the rest of the force were waiting. Croucher was leading the extraction across the dark compound when he felt a wire go tight across his leg. He had accidentally set off a trip-wired booby trap. The armed grenade fell onto the ground beside him. He had no idea how long he had before it exploded,

'I've set this bloody thing off and I'm going to do whatever it takes to protect the others.'
Matthew Croucher

Croucher's prompt and selfless actions had undoubtedly saved his comrades from death or injury. Despite his injuries, he refused to be evacuated, choosing to stay and help engage the enemy forces who came to investigate the scene.

For his swift decision to sacrifice his own life to protect others, Croucher was initially recommended for the Victoria Cross. But as he had not been under enemy fire, he was awarded the George Cross, which he received from the queen on 30 October 2008.

Having completed four tours of duty in the most dangerous war zones in the world, he currently runs a private security firm. He is still a reservist for 40 Commando.

'I lay on top of the grenade for four or five seconds before it exploded. It felt like an eternity.'
Matthew Croucher

roucher's day sack showing the damage done by the grenade. It absorbed much of the force of the blast, nd ended up 30 feet away. (IWM, lent by Matthew Croucher)

ut he did know his comrades were close and in extreme danger. Assessing he situation, Croucher chose to shield the others by throwing himself onto he grenade. It was a choice he believed meant almost certain death for imself. He shouted a warning, then threw himself backwards onto the renade, pinning it between his day sack and the ground. Then he waited. inally it exploded. Amazingly, Croucher was not killed. The blast was nainly absorbed by his day sack and protective equipment. He was thrown hrough the air by the force of the explosion. A lithium battery in the day ack started burning like a flare after being hit by grenade fragments.

Following the explosion Croucher was in pain and disorientated. he only injury in his team was a slight wound on the commander's face.

FIRST RESERVIST TO RECEIVE A GEORGE CROSS SINCE OPERATIONS BEGAN IN IRAQ OR AFGHANISTAN.

WILLIAM BERNARD RHODES-MOORHOUSE VC

26 April 1915

William Rhodes-Moorhouse was adventurous from a young age. He loved speed, neglecting his studies at Harrow and Cambridge in favour of racing motor cars and motorcycles. In 1909, he learnt to fly. A prominent pioneer aviator, he took part in exhibitions, daredevil feats, and air races. He was forced to stop flying following a bad car accident in 1912 but after the outbreak of war in 1914 he immediately enlisted in the Royal Flying Corps.

Initially prohibited from flying due to his old injuries, he was soon back in the air. In March 1915 he was posted to 2 Squadron, based at Merville in France, carrying out reconnaissance and bombing missions. His skilful accomplishment of a number of dangerous missions resulted in him being recommended for promotion to full lieutenant just a month later.

On 22 April, heralded by the first use of gas on the Western Front, the Germans broke the Anglo-French line in front of Langemark. Over the following days, during the Second Battle of Ypres, the Allied line was severely strained. Rhodes-Moorhouse's squadron received orders to bomb three key railway junctions at Roubaix, Tourcoing, and Courtrai to stop German reinforcements from reaching the front.

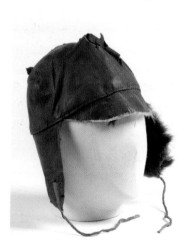

Rhodes-Moorhouse's flying helmet. In 1912, he became the first pilot to fly across the Channel carrying two passengers. The trip was a honeymoon present to his new wife. (IWM)

Rhodes-Moorhouse took off on the afternoon of 26 April in his BE2b bi-plane, to bomb Courtrai, 35 miles behind enemy lines. Flying without his observer to conserve weight, he carried just one 100lb bomb. To place it accurately, Rhodes-Moorhouse had to fly at just 300ft, making him extremely vulnerable to the formidable ground defences. Thanks to his skilful flying the bomb landed perfectly on the railway lines. But the blast rocked the aircraft, and shrapnel hit the wings and rear fuselage. As he tried to regain control, Rhodes-Moorhouse came under attack from the machine guns surrounding the station,

William Rhodes-Moorhouse (1887–1915). His last wish was to be buried on the family estate in Dorset. His son's ashes were interred in the same plot after he was killed during the Battle of Britain in 1940. (IWM, Q 66262)

and the rifles of the gathering soldiers. He received a serious wound to his thigh, but regained control and dived to 100ft in order to gain speed for a climb to safety. As he did so, he was hit in the abdomen and hand. Ignoring the pain of his wounds, and constant dizziness, Rhodes-Moorhouse was

FIRST VICTORIA CROSS AWARDED TO AN AIRMAN.

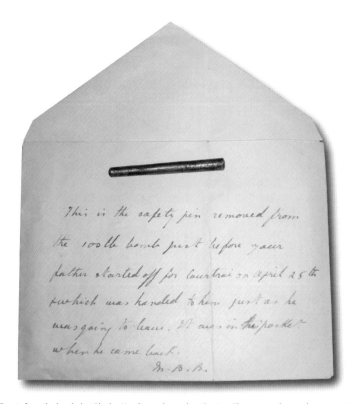

The pin from the bomb that Rhodes-Moorhouse dropped on Courtrai. The note on the envelope was written by his widow. (IWM, LI 2009 999 131 3 3, Courtesy of the Lord Ashcroft Collection)

next day, attended by his friend Flight Commander Maurice Blake, having been informed that he was to be recommended for the DSO.

His action was included in all the official bulletins, and an account was translated into Hindustani for the Indian soldiers who had seen his return flight over the trenches. Back in Britain he was soon regarded as a hero, and there was much support for his action to be recognised. Blake's lobbying resulted in Rhodes-Moorhouse being awarded a posthumous Victoria Cross, gazetted within a month of his death.

'I can't tell you how much we all admire his extraordinary courage in coming down like that to drop the bomb and also in flying the machine back after being hit ... he ought to be given the VC for what he did this afternoon.'
Letter from Maurice Blake to Rhodes-Moorhouse's widow

determined to make the 35-minute return flight to base and make his report.

His fellow pilots on the ground at Merville watched anxiously as he approached the runway at such a low altitude, but his perfect landing gave them hope that he had escaped injury. Once on the ground, it became clear how badly damaged his aircraft was. The cockpit was awash with blood. Despite his injuries and weakness, Rhodes-Moorhouse refused to be taken to a casualty clearing station until he had made his full report. He died the

SACRIFICE

Henry John Andrews VC

22 October 1919

Harry Andrews (1873–1919). (IWM, VC 32)

Harry Andrews was born in 1873, and as a baby was adopted by the Booth family, the founders of the Salvation Army. He went to India at the age of 15 with Emma Booth, wife of Commissioner Booth-Tucker. There, Andrews became the founder of the Salvation Army's medical missionary work. Andrews was desperate to meet the medical needs of those he saw around him, but realised his own limitations due to his lack of formal training. He persuaded a Salvation Army officer trained in medicine to come to India as the first qualified medical officer at the Catherine Booth Hospital in Nagercoil, which he had founded. Andrews was then sent to Anand, in west India, to work as a missionary. He continued to treat those who came to him, and a second hospital was founded. His adoptive brother and the Chief of Staff of the Salvation Army, Bramwell Booth, now sent him to the University of Illinois where he qualified as a doctor. On returning to India, Andrews was sent to Moradabad. There, he designed and supervised the construction of the Salvation Army Hospital, which the Salvation Army later turned over to the government as a war hospital during the First World War for the treatment of sick and wounded Indian soldiers. Andrews was the commandant of the hospital, and he was made MBE for his work. By now he was also married with a family, but he still longed for front line service. He was finally given his chance in 1919, after the war had finished but fighting continued on the North-West Frontier, when he was made a temporary Captain in the Indian Medical Service, and Senior Medical Officer in charge of Khajuri Post, Waziristan.

On 22 October, Andrews heard that an important British convoy had been attacked in the Tochi Valley near the post, and men were wounded. He immediately went to the scene of the attack, which was still under heavy fire, and set up an Aid Post and started to tend casualties. The position he chose gave some protection to the wounded men he was treating, but not to him, and he had to move the post to a safer location. Undeterred by the hostile conditions, he continued to find and bring back the wounded to his aid post, giving them initial attention as he did so. When a van became available, he placed the wounded in the van, so that they could be taken away. Having placed the last casualty in the van, he was about to get in himself, when he was killed. For his selfless actions, he was awarded a posthumous Victoria Cross.

Andrews moving the wounded in Tochi Valley during the Third Anglo-Afghan War. (RAMC)

ANTHONY JOHN GLEDHILL GC

25 August 1966

Tony Gledhill, with wounds received during his action. (IWM, lent by Mr Tony Gledhill GC)

Tony Gledhill was born in 1938. His father was in the RAF and the family moved around a lot during his childhood. Aged 18 he went to Hendon Training School as a police cadet, and became a police constable in the Metropolitan Police in 1957.

Constable Gledhill and his wireless operator Constable Terence McFall were on patrol in their un-armed car in August 1966, when they received a message to investigate a suspicious car. While driving to the location given, the car, containing five members of an armed gang, drove past them at speed. A chase ensued, with the gang's car driving on the wrong side of the road and against one-way traffic at 80 miles an hour. Constable Gledhill managed to keep up with them, even as the men shot at the police car with a sawn-off shotgun and revolvers. The escaping car then crashed into a lorry at a junction. The five men jumped out, and three of them, one carrying a pistol, ran into the yard of a transport contractor. As the police car reached the yard gates, the man carrying the pistol held it to Gledhill's head and ordered both officers to get out of the car, or be shot. They got out, and the man got into the car, hoping to make a getaway. As he reversed, he looked away for a moment, and Gledhill grabbed his gun hand, and as the car moved, got a grip on the car window. The car began to gather speed, but Gledhill held on, being dragged along the road. At this point a tyre burst, the car crashed into some parked vehicles,

Tony Gledhill's medal group. (IWM, lent by Mr Tony Gledhill GC)

and Gledhill was thrown under one of them. Undeterred and despite his injuries Gledhill got to his feet and rushed back towards the police car, but as he went to the driver's door it was flung open, knocking him to the ground. At this point the driver got out of the car, aimed his pistol at the officer and pulled the trigger. But the pistol clicked, empty, and the officers immediately rushed the man, and struggled with him as other police officers arrived. The man was found to have a second pistol in an inside pocket. Both officers had to receive hospital treatment.

Gledhill was awarded the George Cross and McFall the George Medal for their bravery in pursuing and pinning down dangerous men when they knew the high risk of getting injured or killed themselves. Four gang members were sentenced to long prison terms. Gledhill and McFall were praised by the judge in front of the court. Later that year, Gledhill joined the Criminal Investigation Department, serving there for a decade as sergeant. He retired from the Police in 1987.

Norman Cyril Jackson VC

26/27 April 1944

Norman Jackson (1919–94). (IWM, HU 1236)

Norman Jackson was born in Ealing, West London in 1919 and was adopted as a child. At school he developed an interest in engineering, and after leaving school worked as a fitter and turner. In 1939 he joined the RAF Volunteer Reserve. Initially he worked as a fitter, but in 1941 he had the opportunity to join aircrew. After training as a flight engineer, he joined 106 Squadron in July 1943, with the rank of sergeant. The following April, Jackson completed his scheduled tour of 30 operations. However, he decided to volunteer for one more sortie as his regular crew had only performed 29 consecutive operations. He had also just heard that his wife had given birth to their first son, and he decided to celebrate on return from the mission.

After successfully dropping bombs in the target area of Schweinfurt, Jackson's Lancaster bomber was attacked by a night fighter. Despite taking evasive action, the bomber sustained serious damage. A fire broke out near a petrol tank on the starboard wing. Jackson had been thrown to the floor during the encounter and was wounded in the shoulder and leg. Recovering

FIRST RAF FLIGHT ENGINEER TO WIN THE VICTORIA CROSS.

Norman Jackson's medal group. His children had wanted to give his medals to the RAF museum at Hendon, but were eventually forced to sell them. They were sold at auction for a record price in 2004, becoming part of the Lord Ashcroft collection. (Courtesy of the Lord Ashcroft Collection)

quickly, he offered to try and put out the fire on the wing himself. He clipped on his parachute, and carrying a fire extinguisher, climbed out of the cockpit through the escape hatch. Before doing so, he released his parachute so that his crewmates could hold on to it if he slipped. The bomber was flying at 20,000 feet, as Jackson, clinging on in the 200mph freezing slipstream, began to work his way along the fuselage to the wing. He slid down off the fuselage onto the wing, and managed to cling on with one hand while trying to put out the flames with the fire extinguisher. He did manage to quell the flames for a time, but then the German fighter returned.

'The German pilot had seen me and was aiming at the engines…
I was shot off the bloody wing, and they threw my parachute out
of the plane'
Norman Jackson

Jackson's bravery as depicted in *The Victor* comic. Jackson was one of ten Lancaster crew to receive the Victoria Cross during the Second World War. (*The Victor* © D. C. Thomson & Co., Ltd)

The fighter aimed at the engines, so Jackson had to cling on while the aircraft shook. Jackson was wounded, and eventually shot off the wing. He was swept through the flames and over the edge of the wing, his burning, half-inflated parachute trailing behind him. He managed to put out the flames in the parachute with his bare hands, but could not control his descent and landed badly, breaking his ankle. His burnt hands were useless and one eye was closed, so he crawled to the nearest village where

he was taken prisoner. He was paraded through a nearby town to jeers from the local German population before being transported to Dulag Luft. He spent ten months in hospital, but when he recovered he made two escape attempts.

After Jackson's attempt to put out the flames, the captain realised the fire could not be contained, and the six remaining crew abandoned the Lancaster. Four of them survived and were taken prisoner. Jackson's amazing exploits did not become known until after the war when the crew were repatriated. Jackson had not mentioned the incident, but the others unanimously recommended him for a high decoration. He was promoted to warrant officer, and received the Victoria Cross from George VI on 13 November 1945.

Jackson's hands were permanently scarred, but he worked as a salesman for a distillery, and built a house for his family in south-west London. He and his wife had seven children. He was periodically haunted by nightmares of his experience, but reflected that he was more fortunate than comrades who had perished or had struggled to adjust to civilian life. He regularly attended reunions, but was always modest about his astounding actions.

'I'd be scared to walk out on a balcony now. I was young and cocky and thought I could do anything. But I did no more than anyone else would do.'
Norman Jackson, 1969

GEORGE STANLEY PEACHMENT VC

25 September 1915

Born in Lancashire in 1897, George Stanley Peachment was an apprentice fitter engineer when he enlisted in April 1915, giving a false date of birth as he was a month short of 18. He joined the 5th Battalion, King's Royal Rifle Corps as a private. On arriving in France he was sent to the 2nd Battalion, where he was one of the youngest men in his battalion.

His regiment was present for the first day of the battle of Loos, 25 September 1915, the largest assault to date by the British Army on the Western Front. In the preparations for the attack, the company commander, Captain Guy Dubs, made Peachment one of his orderlies.

Following a four-day artillery barrage, and a gas attack on the German lines, the 2nd Battalion went over the top near Hulluch, coughing on the gas which had drifted back towards their own lines. Despite the barrage, German machine guns and barbed wire caused heavy casualties, and the advance halted, then retreated in order to re-organise. Dubs had made it over the wire, closely followed by Peachment, and they got within 15 yards of the German trenches before Dubs was hit in the face by a bomb. Peachment, already slightly wounded, crawled over to help his officer. There

was a shell-hole nearby in which he could have taken cover, but Peachment chose to stay in the open and dress Dubs' wounds. The pair were an easy target, and Peachment was hit by a bomb in the chest, wounding him mortally. Dubs was also shot in the chest. He tried to drag Peachment to the shell hole, but before he could, Peachment was killed by a shot to the head.

Dubs survived, and recommended Peachment for the Victoria Cross. When he was able, he wrote to Peachment's mother, telling her what had happened, and praising her son's bravery.

Peachment's Victoria Cross was presented to his mother by the king at Buckingham Palace in 1916.

'He lost his life in trying to help me and no man could have been braver than he was.'
Letter from Captain G. Dubs to George Peachment's mother

George Peachment (1897–1915). Peachment's body was never recovered, and he is commemorated on the Loos memorial, one of the many thousands who never received an official burial. (IWM, Courtesy of the Lord Ashcroft Collection)

George Peachment's medals. (Courtesy of the Lord Ashcroft Collection)

David George Montagu Hay GC

29 January 1941

David Hay's medal group is unusual because he chose not to exchange his original Albert Medal for the George Cross even though in 1971 all Albert Medals translated into George Crosses. (IWM)

David Hay was born in East Lothian, Scotland in 1921. On leaving Eton, he tried to follow in his father's footsteps and join the Guards, but he was refused. So instead he ran away to sea, joining the Merchant Navy in 1939. He was a cadet with the Blue Funnel Line, serving first with the RMS *Asuturias*, which was torpedoed off Sierra Leone, then the SS *Eurylochus.*

In 1941, the *Eurylochus* was part of a convoy travelling from Liverpool to Takoradi when on the night of 29 January, she was attacked by a German raider. The raider heavily shelled and machine gunned the *Eurylochus*. Many of the crew were killed, and the ship began to go down. Hay manned a 6in gun for as long as possible, an action for which he received the Lloyd's Medal for bravery. The surviving crew did manage to launch two boats, but the rest of the boats were shot to pieces. As the ship went under, the surviving crew jumped and swam for the boats.

The water was full of sharks. Hay managed to get to a raft, but he could see men in the water being viciously attacked by the sharks. Without a thought to his own safety, he dived back into the dark waters to save the stranded Radio Officer. He then managed to swim back to the raft towing the officer, even though a shark attacked him, ripping his clothes.

For his bravery, Hay was awarded the Albert Medal on 29 July 1941. Thirty years later all surviving holders of the Albert Medal had their awards translated into the George Cross. They were all invited to be reinvested with a new GC. Hay chose not to do this but retained his original Albert Medal.

After the action, he joined the Royal Naval Reserve, fed up with being unable to fight back. He was officer in charge of a Naval Police Force in Sierra Leone, and took part in the North African landings. Late in the war he was given command of a minesweeper, HMS *Neave*, which was tasked with blowing up wrecks that were a hazard to shipping.

In later life he fulfilled his love of the countryside by taking over a 2,500-acre estate on the island of Mull. He succeeded to the title of Marquis of Tweeddale and sat in the House of Lords.

RISKING SHARK ATTACK TO SAVE A CREWMATE.

NOEL GODFREY CHAVASSE VC AND BAR

9/10 August 1916; 31 July–2 August 1917

Noel Chavasse (1884–1917). There are more memorials to Noel Chavasse than to any other Victoria Cross winner. (IWM, Q 67309)

Born in Oxford in 1884, Noel Chavasse was one of seven children. He wanted to become a missionary doctor and while studying natural sciences at Oxford, he joined the university's Officer Training Corps. In 1912, Chavasse qualified as a doctor, and alongside his hospital work, he joined the Royal Army Medical Corps, attached to the 10th Battalion King's (Liverpool Regiment), known as the Liverpool Scottish. He quickly became devoted to his territorial regiment, and participated in drill parades, weapons training, sports and summer camps.

When the First World War was declared, the 30-year old Chavasse travelled to London to volunteer for active service as a doctor, accompanied by his twin brother, Christopher, a clergyman who wanted to become an Army chaplain. They both returned to Liverpool where, after a spell examining and vaccinating recruits in Chester, Noel was finally able to rejoin the Liverpool Scottish. In October 1914, the regiment was unexpectedly sent to the front.

Within 24 hours, the regiment had suffered their first casualty, and Chavasse had his own first experience of being under fire, when he went into no man's land to recover the body of a close friend. While he could have stayed at his aid post and sent out stretcher-bearers, Chavasse would choose to go over the top time and again to rescue the dead or wounded.

At Hooge in June 1915, Chavasse worked for 48 hours non-stop to save the wounded, dressing wounds in the trenches, and going into no man's land. When not all the wounded could be carried away to dressing stations he looked after 11 men for a whole day, before returning to no man's land that night to rescue an injured officer and search for other wounded. For this epic display of endurance, Chavasse received the Military Cross. In August 1915, he was promoted to captain and made senior medical officer of the battalion. In September, Chavasse was mentioned in dispatches for working through the night to recover wounded men after an attack at Sanctuary Wood.

In August 1916, the Liverpool Scottish attacked at Guillemont as part of the battle of the Somme. Nearly half the regiment were cut down in one day. Chavasse was out with his stretcher-bearers throughout the attack, not only rescuing wounded but also collecting identification tags from the dead. He got within 25 metres of the German lines and reports indicate that he completely ignored the chaos around him, calmly moving from one shell

The wooden cross that marked Chavasse's grave until after the First World War. A popular officer, he was buried with almost all the survivors of the battalion in attendance. (IWM, LI 2009 999 162 31, Courtesy of the Lord Ashcroft Collection)

CHAVASSE WAS THE FIRST MAN TO WIN TWO VICTORIA CROSSES IN THE SAME CONFLICT. HE IS THE ONLY RECIPIENT OF A POSTHUMOUS BAR TO THE VICTORIA CROSS.

Noel and his twin brother Christopher, both in uniform, in 1915/16. They both excelled in athletics from a young age, and competed in the 1908 Olympics. Christopher later became Bishop of Rochester. (Courtesy of the Lord Ashcroft Collection)

Noel Chavasse's medal group. In total Noel and his three brothers won two Victoria Crosses and three Military Crosses. Chavasse's medals were held by St Peter's College Oxford (founded by his father), until sold to the Lord Ashcroft Collection in 2009. (Courtesy of the Lord Ashcroft Collection)

hole to another. Unbelievably, the only casualty among the stretcher party was Chavasse, who was hit by two shell splinters. His wounds were not serious but he was banned from leaving the dressing station. He spent the next night there treating casualties. He did go and search for a wounded officer, but was caught and admonished. For his actions at Guillemont he was awarded the Victoria Cross, presented to him in February 1917.

On 31 July 1917 the Liverpool Scottish attacked from Ypres in the direction of Passchendaele. Chavasse followed the rapid advance and set up his regimental aid post in a German dugout, which left him exposed to fire from the raging battle. Early in the attack he was hit in the head by a shell splinter. He managed to walk back to a dressing station, but upon being told to wait for further treatment, he went back to his own post. He treated the wounded all day, then that night he went out to search for wounded, and continued to work at his post. Chavasse sustained further head wounds, but despite being in considerable pain, he refused to stop his life-saving work.

At around 3am on 2 August another shell landed near his post, killing or wounding everyone in the dugout. Chavasse was seriously wounded in the stomach. Somehow he managed to get back to the field ambulance. He was taken to a casualty clearing station, and underwent an operation, but died on 4 August. On 14 September it was announced that Chavasse had been posthumously awarded a bar to his Victoria Cross for his actions at Ypres.

'duty called and called me to obey.'
Noel Chavasse, 3 August 1917

Excerpt from a letter written by Chavasse in 1916. (Topfoto)

John Niel Randle VC

4–6 May 1944

John Randle (1917–44). He studied at Merton College Oxford, where he was good friends with Leonard Cheshire, a fellow VC recipient (see pp.110–11). (IWM, HU 2000)

Born in 1917, 'Jack' Randle was called up soon after leaving university shortly before the outbreak of the Second World War. He initially joined the ranks of the East Sussex Regiment, then after Officer Cadet Training he was commissioned into the 2nd Battalion, Royal Norfolk Regiment in June 1942.

In 1944, the Japanese were preparing to launch an offensive against the forces of the British Empire in India. But in April, the Japanese advance was stopped at Kohima, just over the border from Burma, by the 2nd Infantry Division. The next three months saw the British slowly push the Japanese back into Burma through a series of bloody encounters.

On 4 May, at the beginning of the British counter-offensive at Kohima, the 2nd Battalion, Royal Norfolk Regiment were making an assault on GPT Ridge, the southern end of the Japanese position. During the attack, Randle's company commander fell, severely wounded. Randle, temporary Captain, immediately took control of the company and continued the attack. Soon afterwards, he was wounded in the knee by grenade splinters, but he pressed on until the objective was taken. Even when they had taken the crest, and were consolidating their position, he did not rest, instead going out to bring the wounded into the perimeter. His leadership on this day ensured success for his company despite the loss of their commander.

Two platoons were ordered to carry out a frontal attack on the next ridge at first light on 6 May, a position well-protected by Japanese bunkers. Having refused evacuation after his knee wound, that night Randle

Randle's self-sacrifice as depicted on the cover of *The Victor*. His brother-in-law, Leslie Manser, was also awarded a posthumous Victoria Cross, in 1942. (*The Victor* © D. C. Thomson & Co., Ltd)

undertook a risky reconnaissance mission under bright moonlight. The next morning, he led the attack. One of the platoons reached the top of the ridge, taking out a machine gun post, but the other platoon was halted by machine gun fire from a bunker. The bunker had to be destroyed otherwise it would threaten not only the new position of the Norfolks but the lines of communication for the whole battalion. Randle decided to take on the task himself. He charged at the bunker alone, armed with his rifle and bayonet. Running straight at it, he was hit several times. Now mortally wounded, he finally reached the bunker. He threw a grenade into the gun slit, then in a last effort threw himself on to the slit, containing the blast inside the bunker. The machine gun was silenced, and his company, and battalion, went on to take their objectives. Over three days Randle had shown exemplary leadership and initiative, before making the ultimate sacrifice to contain casualties, and aid the success of his company and battalion. For his exemplary actions, he received a posthumous Victoria Cross.

INITIATIVE

'most conspicuous presence of mind'

Difficult situations, which place lives under threat, require quick decisions and clear solutions. Often those who act are not in charge, but they take control. Confident, aware of what needs to be done, they are convinced they can pull it off. No-one else appears to be prepared to act, but someone must. It is their Initiative.

Philip John Gardner VC

23 November 1941

Philip Gardner (1914–2003). While a prisoner-of-war, he raised enough money from fellow prisoners for the victims of the Blitz that it was possible to start the Brunswick Boys' Club in Fulham after the war. Gardner supported the club for the rest of his life. (Courtesy of Dulwich College)

Philip 'Pip' Gardner was born on Christmas Day 1914 and after finishing school trained as an engineer in the family firm. He joined a territorial unit in 1938, and was called up at the outbreak of the Second World War. He was commissioned in 1940 and joined the 4th Royal Tank Regiment in the Western Desert in April 1941.

Two months later, Gardner was in one of two tanks which drove onto an unmarked minefield, joining other stranded tanks. When the commander stood on a mine while inspecting the damage to the tanks, Gardner crossed the minefield four times under fire to help him. When the wounded officer died from his injuries, Gardner assumed command, leading the crews out on foot, then returning the next day to immobilize the tank guns. For this, he received the Military Cross.

In the autumn of 1941, the 4th Royal Tank Regiment took part in the premature breakout from Tobruk. During the fighting on 23 November, Gardner, now an acting captain, was asked to take two tanks to rescue two armoured cars of the King's Dragoon Guards which were out of action and under heavy fire, with their crews in immediate danger. He found the two cars around 200 yards apart, slowly being destroyed by the enemy. Gardner moved his tank close to the nearest car, dismounted and secured a tow-rope to the car. He then saw Lieutenant Beame from one of the armoured cars lying nearby, with his legs blown off. Gardner carefully lifted him into the car, then returned to his tank. The rope broke as the tank started to tow the car, so Gardner went back on foot for Beame. At this point, he was wounded himself in the leg. He managed to carry Beame back to the tank and put him onto the rear deck. He then returned once more to the car to check for other survivors. He was shot in the arm as he climbed back up to the rear deck of the tank, but he held Beame as the tank returned to British lines at top speed, under fire the entire way.

The following year, when the Germans finally took Tobruk, Gardner was taken prisoner-of-war and sent to Italy. He escaped when the Italians capitulated. He evaded capture for four months, until taken prisoner by the Gestapo. He was then sent to Oflag 79, near Brunswick, where he remained until the end of the war. His Victoria Cross was announced while he was a prisoner-of-war, and he was invested by George VI on 18 May 1945.

After the war, he returned to his family firm, becoming the chairman in the 1950s. He spent much of his spare time involved in charity work.

A depiction of Gardner's Victoria Cross action. Despite Gardner's efforts, Beame later died of his wounds. (The National Archives)

JACK HARVEY VC

2 September 1918

Jack Harvey (1891–1940). He is still a local hero in Merstham, and a housing block there was recently named after him. (IWM, VC 545)

Jack Harvey was born in Peckham in 1891. He joined the London Regiment in 1914, and married before going to France the following year in the 1/22nd Battalion. He spent the war on the Western Front, fighting in many of the major battles.

On 2 September 1918, his company were advancing near Peronne when they were held up by intense machine gun fire from a post 50 yards away. Harvey rushed forward on his own, under heavy enemy fire. He charged the post and killed the machine gun crew, shooting two and bayonetting the third. He destroyed the gun, then worked his way along the enemy trench for around 200 yards. Harvey then singlehandedly rushed an enemy dug-out sheltering 37 German soldiers, and forced them to surrender. His quick thinking and bold action allowed the attack to continue, and doubtless prevented heavy casualties for his company. Harvey was recommended for the Victoria Cross, which was presented to him by George V in 1919. His citation noted that he showed courage and determination throughout the entire operation, setting a splendid example to all ranks.

After the Armistice, Harvey returned to his job at George Payne's tea and chocolate works at London Bridge, where he worked for a total of 34 years.

Harvey's action as depicted in *The Victor* comic in 1984, the year his grave was refurbished. (*The Victor* © D. C. Thomson & Co., Ltd)

He died suddenly in 1940, at the age of 48. His widow could not afford a headstone for his grave, and later had to sell her husband's medal. In 1983 Harvey's Victoria Cross went to auction. The purchaser was a policeman who had sold his entire medal collection to be able to afford Harvey's medals. When he discovered that Harvey's grave was unmarked, he and The Queen's Royal Surrey Association arranged for the grave to be refurbished and a headstone set in place. The headstone was dedicated at a service on the 66th anniversary of Harvey's action.

WILLIAM FRASER McDONELL VC

30 July 1857

William McDonell (1829–94). He continued to serve during the Mutiny after his action. (IWM, VC 820)

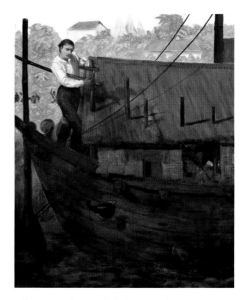

William McDonell cutting the lashing on the boat. He was one of the first two civilians to be awarded the Victoria Cross. The other, Ross Lowis Mangles, saved a wounded soldier on the same day by carrying him six miles across swampy ground, before swimming the river to safety with his charge. (National Army Museum)

William Fraser McDonell was born in 1829, in Cheltenham. Having been educated at Cheltenham College and the East India Company College, he joined the Bengal Civil Service. When the Indian Mutiny broke out in 1857, he was the magistrate of Sarun.

The small garrison of Arrah were besieged by over 2,000 mutinying sepoys in late July 1857. McDonell volunteered to guide a small relief force of around 400 men to Arrah on 29 July. Marching through the night, they eventually came within half a mile of Arrah in the early hours of 30 July. The force was then ambushed just outside the town. McDonell was with the commander of the force, Captain Dunbar, at the time and though they tried to return fire, heavy casualties were taken. Dunbar was shot dead as he stood beside McDonell and McDonell himself was wounded in the leg. At daybreak, the survivors regrouped and it was decided to retreat, as any further attempt on Arrah would be suicidal, with at least a quarter of the force now missing or counted as casualties. It was an arduous 15 miles back to the river where the steamer they had disembarked from was moored, and they were harassed the entire way.

Two miles from safety, the retreating soldiers reached a wide river. The exhausted men found six large boats and with the mutineers bearing down on them, they rushed to get into the boats. McDonell ended up in one of the boats with 35 soldiers. They managed to get the boat into the water, but it just swung back towards the bank and the murderous fire of the sepoys. McDonell realized that the rudder had been lashed. To escape across the river the rope would need to be cut. All the boats were under heavy fire from the bank, but McDonell got a knife, climbed right to the stern of the boat, where he was in full view of the enemy, and, with some difficulty, managed to cut the rope. Two bullets went through his hat, but he received no further injury. He then guided the boat himself across the river, before hitting a sandbank. All but two of the men in the boat then managed to swim to the bank and get to the steamer. His actions certainly saved the soldiers in the boat from being killed.

After the Mutiny, McDonell continued his career in the civil service, finally becoming Judge of the High Court of Judicature at Calcutta. He retired home to Cheltenham, where he died aged 64.

WILLIAM MCDONELL IS ONE OF ONLY FIVE CIVILIANS TO HAVE BEEN AWARDED THE VICTORIA CROSS.

Ishar Singh VC

10 April 1921

Ishar Singh (1895–1963), 28th Punjab Regiment. (IWM, VC 623)

Despite the British success in the initial Waziristan campaign of 1919–20, the Waziris continued to make attacks on British forces into 1921. Ishar Singh, a 25-year old sepoy, was No.1 of a Lewis gun section in a convoy that came under heavy attack in April 1921. Waziri tribesmen ambushed the British force in a narrow gorge near Haidari Kach. The force at the front of the convoy charged the tribesmen, but they came under deadly fire. All the officers were killed and the troops annihilated. The main convoy began to turn back towards the camp. Soon after the attack was launched, Ishar Singh had received a serious gunshot wound in the chest, and collapsed beside his gun. As the fighting became hand-to-hand, the officers of his company were all either killed or wounded, and his gun was taken. Realising how desperate the situation was, Ishar Singh managed to get up, charge the enemy, and take back his gun with the support of two of his comrades. Bleeding heavily, he got the gun back into action. At last reinforcements arrived from the camp. An officer took the gun from Ishar Singh, ordering him to go for medical attention.

Ignoring his orders, Ishar Singh instead went to help the medical officer. He pointed out where the wounded were, and made journeys to a nearby river to get water for them. He took the rifle from a wounded soldier and helped to keep down the fire, and later he stood in front of the medical officer,

ISHAR SINGH WAS THE FIRST SIKH TO WIN THE VICTORIA CROSS.

using his own body as a shield while the medical officer attended a wounded man. Only when he was too weak from loss of blood to object, over three hours later, was he evacuated.

Ishar Singh was presented with his medal in Delhi in 1922 by the Prince of Wales. His was

Ishar Singh's medal group. (Courtesy of the Lord Ashcroft Collection)

one of only five Victoria Crosses awarded between the two world wars. Later awarded the Order of British India, First Class, he is unique in holding both this and the Victoria Cross.

In 1936, Ishar Singh, now a Subedar in the 4th Battalion, 15th Punjab Regiment, was hand-picked to be one of the four King's Indian Orderly Officers; only the most distinguished officers were selected by the Commander-in-Chief for this supreme honour.

Towards the end of his life, Ishar Singh was reportedly financially impoverished, and he either pawned or sold his medal shortly before he died in the Punjab in 1963.

Ishar Singh (back right) with the king's other Indian Orderly Officers in 1936. He was the youngest of the honorary bodyguard for Edward VIII's first, and only, London season. (Courtesy of the Lord Ashcroft Collection)

INITIATIVE

John George Smyth VC

18 May 1915

John George Smyth (1893–1983). When he died in 1983, he was the oldest, and longest-surviving holder of the Victoria Cross. (IWM, HU 56125)

John 'Jackie' Smyth was born in Teignmouth, Devon in 1893. His father had been in the Indian Civil Service, and so it was no surprise that after the Royal Military College, Sandhurst, Smyth was commissioned into the 15th Ludhiana Sikhs, Indian Army, in 1912.

The 15th Sikhs were one of the first Indian battalions to arrive in France, only weeks after the First World War broke out, serving on the Western Front. On 18 May 1915, the 15th Sikhs were on the front line during the battle for Festubert. Lieutenant Smyth was 21, and the battalion's bombing officer.

The previous day a company of the 15th Sikhs supported by a company of the Highland Light Infantry had captured two sections of German trench, only 20 yards from the main enemy force. But the two companies were running out of bombs and ammunition as they desperately tried to hold onto this section of captured enemy ground. Fifteen men of the Highland Light Infantry set off for the reserve trenches to collect more bombs, but none of them got more than half way across the 250 yards of open ground. A group of Highland Light Infantry then set out from the reserve trench to try to relieve the increasingly isolated soldiers, but they too were all killed.

Smyth was now ordered to attempt to reach the 15th Sikhs. He had little confidence that it was possible, but when he called for volunteers, every man in the company bravely stepped forward. Ten were selected, and at 3pm the group climbed over the parapet, carrying two boxes of bombs, in full view of the German trenches. The Germans were ready for them and aimed all their weapons at the party. This actually caused so much turmoil that it gave some cover for the party as they crawled forward, using a demolished trench and the bodies of their comrades for cover. Even so, by the time Smyth reached the end of the old trench, he was accompanied by just one man, Lal Singh, and they had had to abandon one of the boxes. There was a deep stream between them and the forward trench, so the pair had to crawl along it until they found a place to wade across, keeping their precious cargo dry.

Brigadier Sir John Smyth's medal group. Smyth bequeathed his medals to the IWM when he died, however his Victoria Cross is actually a replica, as the original was stolen in a burglary from his house. (IWM, OMD 2718–2733)

JOHN SMYTH WAS THE ONLY INDIAN ARMY OFFICER TO RECEIVE THE VICTORIA CROSS FOR ACTIONS ON THE WESTERN FRONT.

V.C. Hero's Terrible Journey with Bombs

The wonderful story of how Lieut. J. G. Smyth won the V.C. is one of the most inspiring in the annals of the decoration. To relieve the critical position of the 15th Sikhs, Lieut. Smyth and ten sepoys volunteered to convey two boxes of bombs from the reserve trench... Wriggling painfully over the open ground, that literally hissed with a deluge of fire, they hauled the heavy boxes after them. One by one the sepoys were struck, till only Sepoy Lal Singh remained with the Lieutenant. On and on they crawled, over the dead bodies of friend and foe, until they reached their comrades with their precious burden.

Smyth's action, as depicted in the *War Illustrated News*. Smyth's uniform, cap and cane were riddled with bullet holes by the time he reached the trench. (IWM, SmythJ 17363)

Eventually Smyth and Lal Singh reached the trench, shocking the defenders who could not believe anyone had survived the intense fire. Both men were in fact completely unscathed, but Lal Singh was tragically killed by a bullet shortly after reaching the trench. The bombs they delivered enabled the trench to hold out until nightfall. Smyth stayed in the forward trench until night and then he walked back alone across the open ground under the cover of darkness to his trench, where his commanding officer had been told hours before that Smyth was dead along with the rest of his party. Smyth was awarded the Victoria Cross for 'most conspicuous bravery', and his men were all given the Indian Distinguished Service Medal. His act is all the more notable because he had watched the previous two attempts, and had no reason to think that his attempt would be any more successful.

Later in the war he took part in campaigns in Egypt and India. Between the wars he served in Mesopotamia, the Third Anglo-Afghan War and on the North-West Frontier. In total he was mentioned in dispatches six times, and he received the Military Cross for helping to save an ambushed convoy in Waziristan in October 1919 (see Andrews, p.78). In the Second World War he commanded the 127th Infantry Brigade as part of the British Expeditionary Force. After the evacuation from Dunkirk, he then returned to India. During the retreat from Burma, Smyth was in command of 17th Indian Division. He approved the blowing up of a bridge over the Sittang River, which left two-thirds of his division cut off. This was judged to be a mistake and Smyth was relieved of his command. He retired with the honorary rank of Brigadier in November 1942. He spent some years as a military correspondent, and later became a prolific writer, writing on many subjects, including several books on the Victoria Cross and military leadership.

After the war Smyth was a Conservative Member of Parliament for 16 years. In the mid-1950s, he was made a baronet, and a privy counsellor in 1962. Smyth was founder-chairman of the Victoria Cross and George Cross Association in 1956, becoming life president in 1971.

'I didn't think that we had one chance in hell of getting any further than the other people had got, still less as there was no surprise about it at all...'
John Smyth

INITIATIVE

FRANCIS GEORGE MILES VC

23 October 1918

Francis George Miles (1896–1961). (IWM, VC 868)

Francis Miles was born in Clearwell, a village in the Forest of Dean, in 1896. He left school at 13 and became a coal miner. He enlisted in the Gloucestershire Regiment in December 1914, going to France the following September with the 9th Battalion. He was wounded, and after recovering from a poisoned foot, was attached to the 8th Battalion and the Royal Engineers as a tunneller. He was not with the Royal Engineers long as he was wounded in a mine explosion in 1917. He was the only survivor of a team of 50 men buried alive. After convalescence, he rejoined the Glosters, this time the 1/5th Battalion in Italy. He returned to France in the summer of 1918 when the battalion joined the 25th Division.

During the advance against the Bois de l'Évêque near Landrecies, his company was held up by fire from a line of German machine gun posts in a sunken road near the Moulin J. Jacques. Knowing that any delay on his company's part would endanger the whole advance, Miles decided that individual action was needed. He advanced alone for 150 yards, under heavy fire. He located an enemy machine gun, shot the gunner and put the gun out of action. He then saw another post 100 yards further forward. Shooting the gunner, he rushed the gun and managed to capture the eight-man crew. He then stood up, and signalled to his company. Following his signals, they worked around to the rear of the line and captured 16 machine guns, a German officer and 50 men.

German field glasses taken in the VC action and given to Miles. (IWM, LI 2009 999 113 31, Courtesy of the Lord Ashcroft Collection)

For his actions, he was awarded the Victoria Cross. He was received as a hero back home in Clearwell after his investiture by the king. He returned to work in the colliery though he suffered ill-health for most of the rest of his life. In the 1920s he joined the Territorial Army.

He rejoined the Glosters once again two days after Germany invaded Poland in 1939. He served with the 8th (Home Defence) Battalion until he was discharged, medically unfit, the following June. He died, in Clearwell, in 1961.

A heroes welcome: Miles arriving home in Clearwell. It was claimed that Clearwell sent more soldiers to the war than any other village in England in proportion to its size. (IWM, LI 2009 999 113 2, Courtesy of the Lord Ashcroft Collection)

PARKASH SINGH VC
6 & 19 January 1943

Parkash Singh (1913–91) in 1956, when visiting London for the centenary of the Victoria Cross. (Topfoto)

Parkash Singh was born in the Punjab in 1913. Brought up on a small farm, he was rather an unruly boy, though bright and athletic, becoming equal holder of the All-India 800-metre record. He tried to join the Viceroy's Police, but as there were no vacancies he instead enlisted in the 8th Punjab Regiment in 1936.

A tall, somewhat reserved man, he was promoted swiftly. He first saw action on the North-West Frontier and after the outbreak of the Second World War his regiment went to Burma as part of Slim's Arakam offensive in 1942. The rugged terrain meant that the most effective vehicle was the Bren gun carrier, an open-topped tracked vehicle, even though it was not heavily armoured and armed only lightly, with a Bren light machine gun. In early January 1943, the 14th Indian Division, which included Parkash Singh's regiment, was held in a narrow gap between the jungle and the sea at Donbaik on the Mayu peninsula.

On 6 January, two carriers became immobilised while in action. Out of ammunition, they had few options as the Japanese advanced in large numbers to capture them. Havildar Singh, with his driver, advanced in his own carrier and rescued the two crews, under intense enemy fire. Just a few weeks later, on 19 January, three more carriers were put out of action on the beach. In his first rescue, Parkash Singh went out in his carrier to the immobilised vehicle where he found the crew, plus survivors from another disabled carrier. He rescued all the men, and even recovered the weapons from the carrier. He then went out again in his carrier to another disabled vehicle. Under very heavy fire, he dismounted from his own carrier, connected a tow-chain between his own and the stranded carrier, which had two wounded soldiers in it, then towed it to safety.

His actions undoubtedly saved the lives of his injured comrades, and he was presented with the Victoria Cross by the Viceroy, Lord Linlithgow, at the Red Fort in Delhi. Shortly afterwards, Parkash Singh was commissioned as a Jemadar, then Subedar. When he returned home the Punjab government gave him a grant of 64 acres, and a suitable marriage was arranged for him. This turned out to be a happy union, and the couple had four daughters. He became a prosperous farmer, and took an active part in local affairs. He died on a visit to London in 1991.

Parkash Singh's medal group. (IWM, lent by Mrs R. K. Parkash Singh)

Francis Aylmer Maxwell VC

31 March 1900

Francis Maxwell (1871–1917). His family produced many able military leaders, three of his brothers became Colonels of their own regiments, and another was a brigadier general. (IWM, VC 806)

Francis Maxwell was born in 1871 in Surrey. He joined the Royal Sussex Regiment at the age of 20, but moved to the Indian Army Staff Corps in 1893, serving on the subcontinent for the next four years. In 1895, he was sent to relieve the besieged fort of Chitral. During this expedition he recovered the body of a lieutenant-colonel from the battlefield, an act for which he was recommended for a Victoria Cross, but the recommendation was turned down. He then took part in the Tirah expedition of 1897–98, during which he was awarded the Distinguished Service Order. In early 1900, he volunteered to fight in the Boer War, and was attached to Roberts' Light Horse, an irregular unit, as a Lieutenant.

On 31 March, his unit came across a force retreating under enemy attack at Korn Spruit. The Boers had got into the British wagons, and were disarming the soldiers. Maxwell saw that the guns of Q Battery, Royal Horse Artillery, were in danger of falling into the hands of the enemy so he and two other officers decided to try to save the precious guns. Maxwell went out on five occasions, helping to bring in two guns and three limbers, all under

Francis Maxwell's medal group. Nicknamed 'The Brat' by Kitchener, he had a long and distinguished military career with a final rank of brigadier general before being killed on the front line. (Courtesy of the Lord Ashcroft Collection)

heavy fire, with one of the limbers even dragged in by hand. He then went out to try and bring in the last gun, but the attempt had to be abandoned. Maxwell was again recommended for the Victoria Cross, and again it was rejected. But Queen Victoria intervened when she heard that he had been recommended before, and the case was re-examined. Finally Maxwell received his VC, one of five awarded for the action.

Later in the war, Maxwell became an aide-de-camp to Lord Kitchener, with whom he got on very well. Kitchener gave him the nickname 'The Brat'. After the war, Maxwell returned to England with Kitchener, before accompanying him to India. Maxwell then held senior posts in India, Britain and Australia for the next 12 years, including the post of military secretary to the Viceroy of India from 1910.

In May 1916, Maxwell went to the Western Front and took command of the 12th Battalion, Middlesex Regiment. He led them with distinction, earning a bar to his DSO. He was then made brigadier general, in command of the 27th Infantry Brigade. In September 1917, he was shot by a German sniper while carrying out reconnaissance near Ypres.

IAN JOHN MCKAY VC
1/12 June 1982

Ian McKay (1953–82). There are several memorials to McKay including an accommodation barracks at Shrivenham named after him. He was featured on a Falkland Island stamp issued to commemorate the 25th anniversary of the Falklands conflict. (IWM, FKD 2116)

Born in Sheffield in 1953, Ian McKay was a keen sportsman as a boy, excelling particularly in football. He left school at 17, determined to join the Parachute Regiment. He chose not to apply for officer training, but instead work his way up through the ranks. He enlisted in August 1970, and six months later, he qualified as a paratrooper and was posted to 1st Battalion, the Parachute Regiment (1 Para).

His first tour of duty was in Northern Ireland where he was involved in the events of Bloody Sunday. He was wounded and subsequently gave evidence at the inquiry. Over the next decade, McKay worked his way up to the rank of sergeant. By 1982 he was alternating between service with 3 Para, and instructing recruits at Aldershot.

He had just returned to 3 Para, as platoon sergeant for 4 Platoon, B Company, when the Falklands War broke out, and in April 1982, he joined the campaign to re-take the islands from the occupying Argentine forces. His first major engagement was a night attack on Mount Longdon on the night of 11/12 June as part of the final push on Port Stanley. The battle was long and hard, with much hand-to-hand fighting. After reaching their objective, near the top of the mount, McKay's platoon was tasked with clearing the northern side of the ridge. But their advance was stopped by

Ian McKay's medal group. He was described as an outstanding instructor and it was reported after his death that he had been due to go to the Royal Military Academy, Sandhurst. (Courtesy of the Lord Ashcroft Collection)

heavy machine gun fire. The platoon commander ordered the men take shelter, then took a small group, including McKay, forward to probe the enemy positions. When the platoon commander fell wounded, McKay took command. He realised that he had to get the advance moving again so he led an assault on the Argentinean machine gun posts that were holding it up. The three men accompanying him soon fell under the intense fire. McKay charged on alone. Reaching the bunker he threw in a grenade, but he was killed just as the bunker fell silent. McKay lost his own life acting to protect his platoon, some of them teenagers he had trained in Aldershot, and allow the advance to continue. The silencing of the machine guns enabled 4 and 5 platoons to re-form in relative safety, then continue the attack.

McKay's family were informed of his death on the day that the Falklands War ended. His widow was presented with his Victoria Cross at Buckingham Palace on 9 November, and later that month, McKay's body was flown home from the Falklands, and reburied in the military cemetery at Aldershot.

'Mac was the bravest of the brave'
Brian Faulkner

ONE OF ONLY TWO VICTORIA CROSSES AWARDED DURING THE FALKLANDS WAR, BOTH WERE AWARDED POSTHUMOUSLY.

JOHNSON GIDEON BEHARRY VC

1 May & 11 June 2004

Johnson Beharry at the announcement of his Victoria Cross at the Ministry of Defence, 17 March 2005. (IWM, JMOT1 05 1703 1481)

Born in Grenada, Johnson Beharry came to Britain in 1999, and joined the Princess of Wales' Royal Regiment in 2001. After training he became the driver of a Warrior Armoured Fighting Vehicle in C Company, 1st Battalion. He served in Kosovo and Northern Ireland before being deployed to Iraq in 2004.

Early in the morning on 1 May 2004, Beharry was the driver of the platoon commander's Warrior when his company was ordered to replenish an isolated post located in the centre of Al Amarah. Beharry's platoon was the company's reserve force. As the company moved through the dark city, they were ordered to fight through a series of enemy ambushes in order to extract a patrol under heavy attack. Beharry's platoon was then sent in to assist. As they moved through the city, Beharry's Warrior came under ambush and was hit by a number of rocket-propelled grenades. The violent explosions wounded both the platoon commander and the Warrior's gunner. They also damaged the radio meaning that Beharry could not communicate with his turret crew or the other Warriors. Not knowing whether the other men in the vehicle were alive or dead, Beharry decided to move the Warrior forward to try and establish communication. Forced to stop at a barricade the Warrior was again hit by RPGs, which set it alight and filled it with thick smoke. Beharry had to open his hatch to clear his view. Still acting on his own, with no radio communications, he decided the best course of action was to try to drive out of the ambush, leading the other five vehicles. He drove straight through the barricade, suspecting this might set off other explosive devices.

Suddenly, he saw an RPG coming straight towards him. Without stopping, he pulled the hatch closed with one hand, but the explosion forced the hatch open, and the force of the blast further wounded the gunner, and destroyed Beharry's armoured periscope, leaving him no option but to drive for 1.5km with his head out of the hatch, exposed to enemy fire, and still without any communications. As he drove, the vehicle was hit by more RPGs and small-arms fire, and he was hit by a bullet. Eventually he broke clear of the ambush. Identifying another Warrior from his company, he followed it to an outpost, itself under small arms fire.

He stopped the Warrior, and then with total disregard for his own safety, he climbed up to the turret, and pulled first his platoon commander, and then the gunner, out of the burning vehicle, and carried them to a nearby Warrior, before returning to the rear of the Warrior to lead the wounded and disorientated men inside to safety, in total making three trips between

JOHNSON BEHARRY IS THE FIRST RECIPIENT OF THE VICTORIA CROSS IN OVER 20 YEARS.

Johnson Beharry's medal group. Like many modern recipients of the VC and GC, Beharry tends only to wear copies of his medals. This copy set was the one he wore constantly in public between 2005 and 2009. (Courtesy of Johnson Beharry)

Johnson Beharry and Queen Elizabeth II lay a wreath on the tomb of the unknown soldier at a memorial service to mark the passing of the generation of the First World War on 11 November, 2009. (Johnny Green/AFP/Getty Images)

the vehicles, under fire. He then remounted the burning Warrior. He drove it into the defended perimeter of the outpost and immobilised it before finally collapsing from exhaustion in a nearby Warrior. Following medical treatment for his injuries, he returned to duty.

The following month, on 11 June, Beharry's Warrior was lead vehicle of a quick reaction force tasked with cutting off a mortar team that had attacked a base in Al Amarah. As he moved through the dark streets, the Warrior was ambushed from the rooftops. During the initial heavy fire, an RPG exploded on the front armour, just six inches from Beharry's head, inflicting a serious head injury. Other rockets hit the vehicle, wounding the commander and several crew members. Despite blood from his head injury obscuring his sight, Beharry remained in control of the vehicle, and reversed it out of the ambush. It struck the wall of a nearby building, and Beharry then lost consciousness but he had done enough. Other crews could now save the crew of his Warrior. Beharry was seriously injured, spending time in a coma, and undergoing brain surgery. Since the action he has been unable to return to front line duty, and still suffers pain. For his selfless actions, which doubtless saved many lives on these two occasions, Beharry was recommended for the Victoria Cross. He was invested with his medal at Buckingham Palace in April 2005, the first living recipient since 1968. In 2006, Beharry published his autobiography, *Barefoot Soldier*, and was promoted to Lance Corporal.

INITIATIVE

Frederick William Owen Potts VC

21–23 August 1915

Frederick Potts (1892–1943). (IWM, VC 998)

Frederick Potts was born in 1893 in Reading and in 1913 he saved a young boy from drowning in the Thames. In 1915 he left England for the front line as a private in the 1st Berkshire Yeomanry, a mounted territorial unit. The Yeomanry went to Gallipoli, landing in August. Soon after landing, they prepared to make an attack on Scrimitar Hill. Under intense fire from the Turkish positions, and smoke from the burning scrub, Potts' regiment charged up the hill with fixed bayonets.

Potts was shot in his upper left thigh early in the charge. He lay where he fell, camouflaged by the scrub. The regiment took the position, but there were too few of them left to hold it, and they fell back. The Turks retook the trench. Another Reading man from his regiment, Arthur Andrews, managed to crawl to join Potts in his hiding place. Andrews had been shot in the groin and was bleeding heavily. They lay there the whole afternoon, and the whole of the next day, with bullets landing all around, and scrub fires raging in the area. They were both in pain, and suffering from thirst, hunger, and extremes of temperature. They were at risk not only from the continuing Turkish fire, but also from the scrub fires. That night they managed to crawl 300 yards, and took water bottles from their dead comrades, before hiding in a patch of dead ground. Andrews was still bleeding whenever he moved, and Potts did his best to tend the wound with iodine, as Andrews did for Potts. The next night they tried again to move, but Andrews was incapable. Nearby lay a

Left to right: the grandson (Robert Binham) and granddaughter (Anne Ames) of Frederick Potts VC meet the grandson (Chris Andrews), daughter-in-law (Norah Andrews) and granddaughter (Penny Poutney) of Arthur Andrews at the Imperial War Museum on 22 October 2009. The two families met for the very first time at the IWM and their meeting was recorded by BBC Radio Berkshire producer, Graham McKechnie, for a commemorative programme about Potts broadcast on 8 November 2009. Anne Ames is holding Potts' medal group. (IWM, 2009 079 006)

This gold watch was presented to Frederick Potts after his action. It is ornately engraved with his initials while the shovel on the end of the chain serves as a unique reminder of how he dragged Arthur Andrews to safety. (IWM, lent by Mr R. F. Binham)

'When we began to move the Turks opened fire on us; but I hardly cared now about the risk of being shot, and for the first time since I had been wounded I stood up and dragged desperately at the shovel, with Andrews on it.'
Frederick Potts

shovel which had been carried forward to dig new trenches. Potts got Andrews to rest on it, then strapped him on using his equipment, and started to drag him along on it. Potts realised that he would never manage to drag the shovel all the way back if he continued crawling. So he stood up, disregarding his wound and the Turkish fire directed at him, and started to drag Andrews down the hill on the shovel. He had to stop regularly to rest, and neither of them thought they would ever reach the British lines 600 yards away. It took them three hours to reach the bottom of the hill and safety. For staying with Andrews for over 48 hours under fire, then bringing him back to safety, Potts was awarded the Victoria Cross.

He returned to Reading a hero, with a concert in his honour and a dinner given by his colleagues at the engineering works for him. After the war, Potts worked as a tailor with his own shop. He was in the Home Guard during the Second World War until his death in November 1943.

POTTS WAS THE FIRST YEOMANRY VICTORIA CROSS.

WILLIAM COSGROVE VC

26 April 1915

William Cosgrove (1888–1936). (IWM, VC 269)

Born in County Cork in 1888, William Cosgrove was an apprentice butcher before he joined the Royal Munster Fusiliers. When war broke out in 1914, Corporal Cosgrove was stationed with the 1st Battalion in Burma. They returned to England in early 1915 and prepared for the Gallipoli landings.

The Royal Munster Fusiliers were part of the covering force landed on V Beach, east of Cape Helles at Gallipoli, from the SS *River Clyde* (see pp. 25–7). The landing was fiercely opposed by the Turks, and heavy casualties were suffered with around 100 of the 1st Battalion killed or wounded. Despite their withering fire, the Turks did not force the invaders off the beach but did manage to prevent the Fusiliers from moving off into the village of Sedd-el-Bahr. Pinned on the beach the survivors were held back by the devastating fire and the copious amounts of barbed wire which the naval bombardment had failed to destroy.

The day after the landings, it was clear that the British needed to capture the village. As the line moved forward part of the attack dealt with the thick wire entanglements alongside the fortified position. Cosgrove was one of the group of men detailed to destroy the wire. The officer leading them was quickly killed so Cosgrove took charge, and led the men, under heavy fire, up to the wire. Using cutters they tried to cut through the entanglements, but it had little effect. So Cosgrove, a tall, strong man, affectionately known as the 'East Cork Giant', grabbed the nearest post and pulled it out of the ground single-handedly. When they saw what he was doing, the other men

THE EAST CORK GIANT'S BRAVERY AT GALLIPOLI.

Cosgrove tearing up the barbed wire supports on Gallipoli. (Courtesy of the Lord Ashcroft Collection)

began cheering. He continued to pull up posts despite the heavy fire and men falling all around him. His actions enabled the wire to be cleared. Later in the fighting that day, Cosgrove was seriously wounded by machine gun fire, but continued to fight on. He underwent two operations in Malta, and made a partial recovery from his wounds.

For his actions, he was awarded the Victoria Cross, and was decorated at Buckingham Palace on 4 November 1916. He was said to be a shy man who hated to be fussed over.

He continued his career in the Army after the war and spent six years in Rangoon before retiring in 1934. However his Gallipoli wounds had left him with recurring health problems, which cut short any plans for retirement. He died in Millbank Hospital, London, in 1936. His body was returned to Ireland for burial.

'I believe there was wild cheering when they saw what I was at, but I only heard the screech of bullets and saw dirt rising all round from where they hit. I could not tell you how many I pulled up. I did my best and the boys around me were every bit as good as myself.'
William Cosgrove

ENDURANCE

'exceptional perseverance and a high devotion to duty'

There is something unending about Endurance, like a giant Sequoia tree reaching up into infinity or the pendulum of a clock ticking without end. It is the opposite of Aggression. It is all about 'cold courage', about knowing the cost and being prepared to pay it. It involves mental and physical resilience, not giving in and rising above the pain.

John Rouse Merriott Chard VC
Robert Jones VC

22–23 January 1879

John Chard (1847–97). He had served in the Corps of Royal Engineers for over a decade before Rorke's Drift, but had never before seen action. (IWM, VC 204)

Robert Jones (1857–98). The Welshman worked on the land, then joined the Army three years before Rorke's Drift. (IWM, Q 80549)

In January 1879, the British invaded Zululand. On the advance, a depot was established at Rorke's Drift, an old Swedish mission station. The store and makeshift hospital there were protected by a company of the 2nd Battalion, 24th Regiment as well as a company of the Natal Native Contingent (NNC), a total of 400 men.

On 22 January, a huge Zulu army destroyed part of the British main column at Isandlwana. The men at Rorke's Drift were warned by fleeing survivors that the Zulus were coming. The most senior officer was 31-year-old Lieutenant John Chard. He and Lieutenant Bromhead, in command of the men of the 2nd Battalion, 24th Regiment, decided to make a stand. Chard ordered the two buildings fortified, and barricades built between them using biscuit boxes and mealie (local corn) bags. Before the battle, the NNC company fled, leaving Chard with just 150 men. He hastily ordered another wall built across the yard to allow the defenders to pull back to a smaller area if necessary.

At 4pm, around 4,000 Zulus surrounded the mission. Soon the defenders were using their rifles and bayonets to defend the makeshift walls against the constant Zulu charges as Zulu snipers kept up heavy fire from the nearby hill. After two hours, the defenders had to fall back to the smaller enclosure, leaving the hospital completely cut off.

Private Robert Jones was one of the six soldiers posted in the rooms of the hospital to defend the building and the few soldiers too sick to fight. He was stationed in a room at the rear of the hospital, with a barricaded external door and window. Despite the efforts of the soldiers and armed patients, the Zulus got right up to the walls, set the roof alight, and started to break in. The defenders had to knock holes in the partition walls to escape from room to room. Having used all his ammunition, Jones helped one patient into the adjoining kitchen, before returning to bayonet warriors forcing their way through the barricaded door. Jones had received three assegai wounds during the struggle.

The high window in the hospital's kitchen was now the only way of escaping to the yard. Jones, along with the three other surviving soldiers saved 14 patients from the hospital, moving them from room to room, and out of the kitchen window, fighting off attacking Zulus all the while. Jones was the last to leave. He made one final attempt to save a delirious patient who had refused to leave his bed, but found Zulus stabbing him where he lay. As Jones dropped out the window, the roof collapsed.

In the enclosure, Chard worked hard to keep up morale. He had a redoubt built of mealie bags in the centre, providing shelter for the wounded, and a better field of fire. The light of the flames from the burning

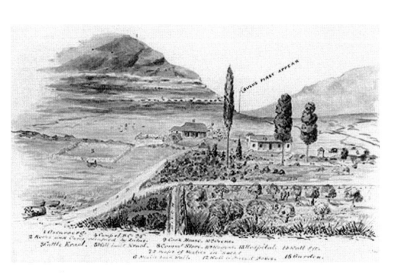

A labelled sketch of Rorke's Drift drawn by Chard. Rorke's Drift is one of the most famous final stands in military history, and its defenders are often seen as the epitome of the stalwart British infantryman, fighting to the very last against impossible odds. (Courtesy of the Lord Ashcroft Collection)

John Chard's medal group. Chard never married, but it is rumoured that he gave his original Victoria Cross to one of Queen Victoria's ladies-in-waiting. (Courtesy of the Lord Ashcroft Collection)

hospital allowed the defenders to use their rifles until around 10pm, when they had to resort to bayonets. At around midnight, after eight hours of fighting, the attacks began to tail off. Zulu fire continued until 4am, but dawn revealed the Zulus were retiring. Chard ordered patrols out, and the defences strengthened, ready for another attack. Work stopped when the Zulus suddenly reappeared, but they disappeared again as the column arrived from Isandlwana.

At Rorke's Drift, Zulu casualties were estimated to have been at least 600, if not closer to 1,000, while the stoic defenders sustained just 25 casualties. Eleven Victoria Crosses were presented to the defenders, seven to soldiers of the 2/24th. Mentioned in both the official battle report, and

Chard's account for the queen, Jones was awarded the Victoria Cross for his bravery in the hospital. He was discharged from Army service in 1888. He found work as a labourer on an estate, and he and his wife had five children. However, one of his wounds had left him with head pains, and in 1898, he collapsed, and started to act strangely. A few weeks later, at the age of 41, he committed suicide.

For his instrumental role in preparing the defences of the mission, and his work throughout the defence, inspiring and leading the defenders, Chard was awarded the Victoria Cross, and promoted to captain and brevet major. The citation for Chard and Bromhead notes that the success of the defence was in large part due to the actions of these two men.

ODETTE MARIE CÉLINE SANSOM GC

April 1943–May 1945

Odette Sansom was born in France in 1912. When she was six, her father was killed at Verdun, just days before the Armistice. In 1931, she met and married an Englishman, Roy Sansom. The couple moved to England and had three daughters. When the Second World War broke out, her husband joined up. In 1942, Odette responded to a radio appeal by the Admiralty for photographs of France, and was asked to the War Office for an interview. After a second interview she was invited to join the Special Operations Executive and return to France

Odette Sansom's medal group. She was awarded the Légion d'Honneur in 1950. Her medals were stolen in 1951, but returned after an appeal was made by her mother. (IWM, OMD 3945–3953)

Odette Sansom (1912–95), codename *Lise*. (IWM, HU 3213)

as a secret agent. Leaving her young daughters, she joined the Women's Transport Service (First Aid Nursing Yeomanry) as a Lieutenant and began training. The first four attempts to insert her to France by plane failed, and she eventually got there via Gibraltar, arriving in November 1942. She was intending to make her way to a resistance ring near Auxerre, but she was delayed in Cannes, where she worked with a British agent, Peter Churchill. The German invasion of Vichy France forced her to remain there, and for six months she worked undercover in Cannes and at St Jorioz in the

Alps, narrowly evading capture on several occasions. In April 1943, her luck ran out. She and Churchill were betrayed by a double agent and handed to the Gestapo. Initially she was held and interrogated by the Germans in Fresnes Prison, Paris. They pulled out all her toenails and burnt her back with a red-hot iron, but even under torture she refused to give away the hiding place of other British agents. She also improved Peter Churchill's treatment by keeping to a cover story that Peter was related to Winston Churchill, she was his wife, and that he was only in France on her insistence. While at the prison, she was brought before a tribunal and sentenced to death on two counts, for being a British secret agent, and for being a Frenchwoman guilty of crimes under German occupation law.

In 1944 she was sent to Ravensbrück concentration camp. For over three months she was kept in a pitch-black, underground cell, then later moved to a cell near the camp crematorium. There, still in solitary confinement, she could not avoid hearing what was happening to the majority of detainees in the camp. She was later moved to the hospital block, suffering from

FIRST WOMAN TO RECEIVE THE GEORGE CROSS DIRECTLY, AND THE ONLY WOMAN NOT TO RECEIVE IT POSTHUMOUSLY.

uberculosis, and so escaped the execution order sent out from Berlin in early 1945 which led to the murder of fellow SOE agents.

In April 1945, the camp commandant, still believing her to be related to Churchill, tried to save his own life by taking her to the American lines, but upon arrival she promptly denounced him, and stood witness against him and other camp staff at the Nuremburg trials. At the end of her ordeal, she weighed less than 6 stone, had tuberculosis and an injured spine. She was one

The jacket that Sansom wore in Fresnes prison and Ravensbrück camp. (IWM, UNI 11957)

A rag doll made by Odette, during her incarceration at Fresnes. She gave it and another to the German padre at the prison. His family returned them to her after the war. (IWM, EPH 4082)

Sansom with Peter Churchill and her daughters immediately after her investiture at Buckingham Palace. The couple married in the late 1940s but divorced in the 1950s. Sansom later married Geoffrey Hallowes, also an SOE veteran. (Topfoto)

of only 13 female agents in France, and the only woman agent on the death list, to survive the war.

In 1945 Sansom was made MBE, and the following year she was awarded the George Cross. She felt that the award was made to her on behalf of all the agents who had gone to France, and who had suffered even more than she had. A few years later a book and film were produced about her story. Both had her cooperation because she wanted to honour those who hadn't come home. In later life she was on the committee of the Victoria Cross and George Cross Association. She died in 1995.

ENDURANCE

STEPHEN GEORGE STYLES GC

20 & 22 October 1971

George Styles grew up in Sussex. He won a place to study at university, but was called up for national service. In 1947 he was commissioned into the Royal Army Ordnance Corps. He then decided to make his career in the Army. He trained as an ammunition technical officer, and studied for a degree in engineering followed by further training in bomb disposal.

In 1969, Styles was deployed to Northern Ireland where he led the team of experts who worked to counter the terrorist bombing campaign from the outset of the Troubles. The bombmakers were constantly trying to outwit the disposal experts by developing increasingly complex bombs. In October 1971, Major Styles was called to defuse a bomb at the Europa Hotel in Belfast. The bomb, containing 10–15lb of explosive, had been left in the public telephone box in the bar. On examining the bomb, Styles realised that it was similar to a new type of bomb that had recently killed one of his colleagues. He discovered that it was fitted with anti-handling devices, meaning that the slightest movement would set it off until the electrical circuit had been neutralised. Assisted by two RAOC officers, Styles carried out a seven-hour operation to disarm and remove the bomb. The work had to be carried out in stages, each preceded by careful planning. He took great personal risks in order to reduce the danger to his team. Eventually he was able to put a line around the bomb, and carefully pull it out of

George Styles (1928–2006). He was fascinated by mechanics and munitions from a young age. (IWM, GC 390)

Styles' uniform jacket. He was influential in the development of the remote-controlled device for dealing with bombs, known as the 'Wheelbarrow'. (IWM, UNI 11038)

George Styles' medal group. (IWM, by permission of Mrs J. R. F. Bugden)

the hotel and onto the pavement.

Styles thought he knew who the bombmaker was, and felt it likely that the man would try again. Sure enough, two days later Styles was called back to the Europa to deal with another bomb, this time on the main reception desk, and containing almost 40lb of explosive. The bombmaker had made this bomb even more complex than the last. Scrawled on the bomb were the words 'Te-hee, He-Hee, Ho-Ho, Ha-Ha'.

Styles and his men worked intensely for nine hours in the greatest of personal danger to disarm, remove and dismantle this larger bomb. Styles' calm demeanour and skill contributed to the successful outcome of both operations. He was awarded the George Cross, and was presented with it by Elizabeth II in March 1972.

After his time in Northern Ireland, Styles was appointed Chief Ammunition Technical Officer, responsible for the RAOC bomb disposal teams throughout the world. Styles retired from the Army in 1974, and spent years campaigning for a change in the design of commercial detonators in order to preclude their use in improvised explosive devices (IEDs).

'You couldn't avoid the feeling of menace each time you walked towards that telephone box. Inside it was enough energy to blow your head from your shoulders, your arms and legs from your trunk, and your trunk straight through the plate glass windows of the Europa.'
George Styles

DOREEN ASHBURNHAM GC

23 September 1916

Doreen Ashburnham (1905–91) with Anthony Farrar, both wearing their medals. (IWM, by permission of Djinn Ruffner)

Doreen Ashburnham was born in Sussex in 1905. Shortly before the First World War her father moved the family to an estate at Cowichan Lake, Vancouver Island. In 1916, when she was 11 years and 4 months old, she and her 8-year-old cousin, Anthony Farrar, were on their way to ride their ponies when they were attacked by a cougar. The cougar was reported to be over 7 feet tall, though probably partly blind. The cougar first attacked Doreen, landing on her back and knocking her down, biting and chewing at her. Anthony bravely attacked the animal with the bridle he was carrying. It moved off and the two children forced it back, brandishing their bridles. The cougar then leapt at Anthony, severely injuring him, and almost scalping him. Doreen realised that if she used her bridle to attack the cougar, she might further injure Anthony. So instead she jumped on the animal's back, and hit it round the head with her bare hands, putting her right arm into its mouth to stop it biting the young boy. The cougar reared up over Doreen, but then gave up the struggle. The children, dazed and badly injured, managed to get home, where Doreen's parents raised the alarm. A neighbour then shot the cougar, which was later stuffed and displayed. Anthony needed 175 stitches to his head, and spent a long time in hospital, while Doreen suffered blood poisoning.

The story of the children's heroism had great appeal, and was widely reported not only across North America, but also in England. In December 1917, it was announced that both children would receive the Albert Medal. Doreen was the youngest female recipient, and Anthony the youngest ever recipient.

In 1925 Doreen left school, and came to England as a debutante. She then returned to California, where she had previously wintered with her family. She lived a full and varied life, becoming a member of the first women's polo team in the United States, and breeding horses which she rode in international competitions. She also learnt to fly, and loved fast cars. She married in 1945, and had a daughter.

Holders of the Albert Medal were invited to exchange their medals for the George Cross in 1971, and in 1974 she received the George Cross. Anthony Farrar, however, did not survive to exchange his. He had been killed, aged 22, while on manoeuvres with his regiment in Canada in 1930. Active until the end, Doreen was still driving sports cars in her eighties. She died in California in 1991.

Doreen Ashburnham's medals. (IWM)

THE YOUNGEST-EVER FEMALE RECIPIENT OF A BRITISH GALLANTRY AWARD.

Geoffrey Leonard Cheshire VC

1940–44

Born in 1917, the son of an academic lawyer, Leonard Cheshire joined the Oxford University Air Squadron while studying law at Oxford. He joined the RAF with a permanent commission after his graduation in June 1939. After flight training school he was posted to 102 Squadron, Bomber Command.

He completed four tours of duty as a pilot in Bomber Command. His first tour saw him flying missions over the Ruhr. On one of his missions, a shell burst inside his aircraft, blowing out one side and starting a fire, yet he still continued on to bomb his target. For this he was awarded the DSO. He also undertook a number of convoy missions. Once his tour finished, he immediately volunteered for a second tour, carrying out bombing raids on Berlin, Bremen, Cologne, Duisberg, Essen and Kiel. In 1941, he married an American actress, Constance Binney, after a whirlwind romance. Constance encouraged her husband to write about his experiences, and his book *Bomber Pilot* quickly sold out its first print run.

In his third tour of duty, he took command of 76 Squadron and led them on a number of missions before becoming the youngest group captain at the age of 25, and being appointed as station commander at Marston Moor in March 1943. However, he missed operations, and relinquished his rank to return to flying, completing a fourth tour in command of the legendary 617 Squadron, the Dambusters. By this time, Cheshire held a DFC, and two bars to his DSO, and was one of the most highly decorated men in the RAF.

During this tour he pioneered a new pathfinding method where a low-flying aircraft would drop flares at very low heights to mark targets for the following bomber force. He led his squadron personally on every mission, pathfinding alone at a very low level. After testing his method at Limoges in early 1944, he and his squadron put other precision targets out of action including the submarine pens at Le Havre, and the V-weapon sites.

In 1944, Cheshire received the Victoria Cross. The citation is unusual because the medal was awarded for his bravery over 100 missions and four

Leonard Cheshire (1917–92) photographed in November 1944 shortly after arriving in India. (IWM, CI 842)

Leonard Cheshire with his air and ground crews at Linton-on-Ouse where he served his second tour of operations with 35 Squadron. (IWM, CH 6373)

CHESHIRE IS THE ONLY AIRMAN TO BE AWARDED THE VICTORIA CROSS IN THE SECOND WORLD WAR FOR A PERIOD OF GALLANTRY RATHER THAN SINGLE ACTION.

eonard Cheshire's medal group. (IWM, OMD 3700–3709)

years, though it specifically noted the raid on Munich in April 1944, a target he chose to test his pathfinding method on because of its formidable defences. His citation concludes that he had 'a reputation second to none in Bomber Command'. He was an inspirational figure, having managed to maintain and hone his operational ability and skill over four years of gruelling operations.

After his hundredth mission, Cheshire was grounded, serving in staff positions in South East Asia and America. The strain of the last few years was now beginning to tell on Cheshire, but his war was not yet over. In 1945 he was the Prime Minister's special observer when the atomic bomb was dropped on Nagasaki. His health continued to deteriorate and he was invalided out of the RAF in 1946.

After the war, Cheshire started a scheme for communities of ex-servicemen. This collapsed, leaving him with a large empty house. When he heard that one of the servicemen had terminal cancer, he housed him and nursed him until his death, by which time others had come to him, and soon the house had 24 occupants. This ultimately led to the charity now known as Leonard Cheshire Disability, an international organisation housing and caring for the disabled. His tireless humanitarian work, which continued even during his hospitalisation for TB, was inspired by his Roman Catholic faith, developed following the war. In the course of his charitable work he met and married his second wife Sue Ryder, wartime member of the Polish section of the SOE, and founder of the Sue Ryder foundation.

He also founded the World Memorial Fund which led to the creation of the National Memorial Arboretum. Towards the end of his life, Cheshire accepted official recognition of his achievements, becoming a member of the Order of Merit in 1981, and elevated to the peerage in 1991. He died from the effects of motor neurone disease in 1992, aged 74. Either his wartime service or his humanitarian work would have made him one of the most remarkable men of our times.

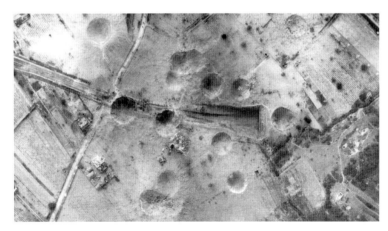

This photograph shows the aftermath of 617 Squadron's bombing raid on the southern entrance of the Saumur railway tunnel on 8/9 June 1944. Cheshire marked the target personally for this mission, the first time the 12,000lb Tallboy bomb was used operationally. The accuracy of the bombing can be seen by the 18 craters within 220 yards of the tunnel mouth. (IWM, HU 92978)

ERNEST HERBERT PITCHER VC

8 August 1917

Ernest Pitcher (1888–1946) painted in 1918, by Ambrose McEvoy. The son of a coast guard, Pitcher was born and grew up in Cornwall. He was one of the few regular Royal Navy men on Campbell's ships. (IWM, ART 1327)

Ernest Pitcher's medal group. He received the French Medaille Militaire and the Croix de Guerre for the same action as his Victoria Cross. He was formally invested in December 1917. He retired from the Navy in 1927 with the rank of chief petty officer following 25 years' service. (Courtesy of the Lord Ashcroft Collection)

Ernest Pitcher joined the Navy at the age of 15 in 1903. In 1915, he volunteered for service in the Q-ship fleet. Q-ships were merchant ships with concealed weaponry which tried to lure U-boats into making surface attacks. It was secret and dangerous work. After Pitcher volunteered for service on the Q-ships he joined one of the most illustrious vessels, HMS *Farnborough* under Lieutenant-Commander Gordon Campbell. Campbell was rapidly establishing himself as one of the geniuses of this war of deception and successfully sunk a U-boat while in command of the *Farnborough*. When Campbell moved onto his next command, HMS *Pargust*, Pitcher followed him. After *Pargust* successfully sank a U-boat, a ballot was held and two VCs awarded. Pitcher received a DSM. Next Pitcher followed Campbell once again to HMS *Dunraven*.

On 8 August 1917, a U-boat closed with the *Dunraven* around 130 miles off Ushant, in the Bay of Biscay. Petty Officer Pitcher was the captain of the concealed 4in after-gun at the rear of the ship. The first part of the plan went perfectly. The U-boat opened fire, so the *Dunraven* sent off a distress signal and fired its 'merchant ship' gun, boiler trouble was simulated by releasing steam, and a party of men 'evacuated' by boat.

The submarine then scored three hits in quick succession. The first shell cut communications between the gun crew and the bridge. If the gun crew moved, it would give away the game, so they stayed where they were. But the other shells started a fire on the poop deck. Pitcher and his crew were stuck on a red-hot deck, over an ammunition store. The crew lifted the boxes of cordite on to their knees to try to prevent them exploding, and waited in the heat.

Before Campbell had another chance to target the U-boat, the inevitable explosion in the ammunition store blew out the stern of the ship and threw the gun and crew in the air. Pitcher landed on mock railway trucks made of wood and canvas, which saved his life.

Campbell continued the duel until the U-boat, undamaged but out of torpedoes, dived as other British and American ships approached. For the action off Ushant, a ballot was held to choose one recipient for the Victoria Cross from the officers, and one for the crew, and the outstanding gallantry of the after-gun crew was recognised by the selection of Pitcher for the honour.

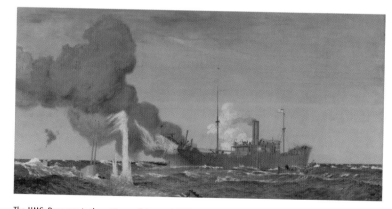

The HMS *Dunraven* in the action on 8 August 1917, painted by Charles Pears. Afterwards, the *Dunraven* had to be abandoned due to damage. Campbell and his crew were bitterly disappointed when they learnt that she would not be replaced as the Q-service was wound down. (IWM, ART 5130)

ERIC CHARLES TWELVES WILSON VC

11–15 August 1940

Eric Wilson (1912–2008). Wilson was told of his 'posthumous' medal by a captured RAF officer while a prisoner-of-war in Eritrea. (IWM, LD 2572)

A depiction of Wilson defending the Tug Argan Gap. When he regained consciousness after the battle he found himself surrounded by dead bodies, including that of his terrier. (National Archives)

Following the Royal Military College, Sandhurst, Eric Wilson was commissioned into the East Surrey Regiment in 1933. In 1937 he volunteered for secondment to the King's African Rifles, and served in Tanganyika until he secured a second secondment to the Somaliland Camel Corps in 1939, where he formed Somali conscripts into a company of machine gunners. He formed deep attachments with his men, and was a fine commander.

When Mussolini's troops invaded British Somaliland in 1940, the Camel Corps fought to delay the advance. Captain Wilson was commanding the Camel Corps machine gun company. He placed the Vickers machine guns on the four small hills of the Tug Argan Gap. After briefing his men, he joined the forward-most position on Observation Hill, where he remained at the forefront of the defence for four days.

The Italian attack began on 11 August with an artillery bombardment of Wilson's position. The Vickers was blown off its tripod, but was undamaged. Wilson was wounded severely in the shoulder and eye, and his spectacles were destroyed. That day saw heavy incoming fire, and small attacks along the defences. Despite suffering from acute malaria as well as his wounds, Wilson remained at the exposed position through another day of probing attacks until on 13 August, the Italians finally made a large-scale assault. They overran the British artillery position and renewed fire on Wilson's machine gun posts. On 15 August two of his guns were blown to pieces, and many of his men lay dead around him. An order to withdraw was sent to his position, but it never arrived. Wilson stayed with his gun until the position was overrun. He was thought killed, and a recommendation was put forward for a posthumous Victoria Cross.

But Wilson hadn't died, he had been taken prisoner following the battle. He underwent medical treatment for his wounds and illness before being sent to a prisoner-of-war camp. His posthumous Victoria Cross was gazetted two months later. He and the other prisoners had almost completed a tunnel for a mass escape attempt when they woke one morning in April 1941 to find their guards gone and the camp liberated.

On his release, Wilson volunteered to use his knowledge of the desert in the Long Range Desert Group. Later in the war he was second-in-command of a battalion in Burma. After suffering scrub typhus he spent the last months of the war commanding an infantry training centre in Uganda. Wilson left the Army in 1949 and joined the Overseas Civil Service in Tanganyika staying there until 1961.

Wilson chose to keep in touch with the families of his Somali soldiers. He was honorary secretary of the Anglo-Somali Society for a number of years, and organised relief for the victims of the famine that struck Somalia in 1975. He sold his Victoria Cross in 2005, and used part of the money to set up a centre for UK-based Somalis. His youngest son Hamish maintained the family link, fighting with the sons of the men his father had fought beside, in the war to establish a separate state of Somaliland in 1991.

FIRST VICTORIA CROSS IN THE AFRICAN CAMPAIGNS IN THE SECOND WORLD WAR.

ENDURANCE

FOREST FREDERIC EDWARD YEO-THOMAS GC

1943–45

Tommy Yeo-Thomas (1901–64) in RAF uniform. After each of his trips to France the BBC would include in its French transmission the message, 'Le lapin blanc est rentre au clapier (The White Rabbit has returned to his hutch)'. (IWM, HU 98898)

Forest Yeo-Thomas, known as Tommy, was born in 1901 in London, but spent his youth in France as his family had been settled there for a century. Though underage he was determined to take part in the First World War, and became a dispatch rider late in the war with the American Army. In 1919–20, he joined the American Legion fighting with the Poles against the Bolsheviks.

On his return to France he undertook various jobs, and in 1932 started work at the fashion house Molyneux, where he eventually became a company director.

When the Second World War broke out he tried to enlist, but the years he had added to his age in the First World War now worked against him. Eventually he managed to join the RAFVR and served with the Advance Striking Force. He was in one of the last boats to leave France after its fall. In October 1940 he was commissioned as an intelligence officer. He was determined to return to occupied France and managed to get himself taken into the Special Operations Executive. Operations in France were directed by two main sections, F and RF. Yeo-Thomas was made responsible for planning in the RF section, linked to the Free French and working to bring

together all the small pockets of resistance in France. He was given the codename *The White Rabbit* and the rank of Wing Commander.

In February 1943 he made his first trip to France where, with Andre Dewavrin and Pierre Brossolette, he worked to unite the various resistance groups. Also during his trip he aided a French officer who was being followed by the Gestapo, and brought back with him a wounded American airman. In September he returned to continue his work with the Maquis, narrowly evading arrest six times. After his second trip he successfully petitioned Winston Churchill for supplies and weapons for the resistance in France.

In February 1944, Yeo-Thomas heard that Brossolette had been captured, and arranged to be parachuted into France to try and help him escape. But the Germans were on the look-out for *The White Rabbit*, and he was arrested outside a Paris metro station in early March. He was tortured and interrogated continuously for four days, then ongoing over two months. The Gestapo tried 'the bath': chaining him up and immersing him upside down in freezing cold water and beating him, but he refused to tell them anything. The chains cut into his arms and legs, and he nearly lost an arm to blood

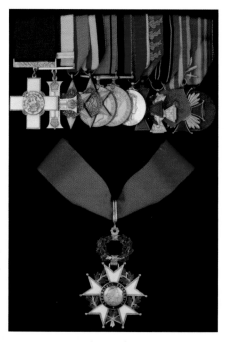

Forest Yeo-Thomas' medal group. (IWM, OMD 2431–2443)

114

poisoning. He then underwent four months of solitary confinement at Fresnes prison, Paris, beaten every morning. After it was discovered he was getting news into the prison he spent three weeks in a pitch-black cell with almost no food, singing patriotic songs to infuriate his captors. He made two unsuccessful escape attempts, and after D-Day, he was sent to Compiègne, and then to Buchenwald concentration camp with 36 other prisoners. Sixteen of them were executed. Realising that he was high on the list for execution, he managed to swap his identity with that of a French prisoner dying of typhus and later organised a small resistance effort within the camp.

Under his new identity he was transferred to a work commando at a satellite camp, Rehmsdorf. In April 1945, the prisoners were moved once again by train. During the journey he organised an escape, and he was one of ten who managed to get away. Starving and desperately weak, he was captured by German troops just 800 yards from the American lines. Posing as an escaping French Air Force prisoner-of-war he was sent to another camp, where he organised yet another escape attempt with some French prisoners. He collapsed during the escape, but with assistance, he reached the advancing Americans.

For his fierce spirit and resistance over such a long period, he was awarded the George Cross, the Military Cross and bar, the Polish Cross of Merit, the Croix de Guerre, and the Légion d'Honneur.

His health was permanently damaged by his ordeals, yet he helped to bring several Nazi war criminals to trial. He then returned to Molyneux, but ill-health forced him to resign. The legacy of his wartime sufferings never left him, and he died in 1964, aged 62, on the 21st anniversary of his first drop into France. A best-selling memoir of his wartime exploits, *The White Rabbit*, by Bruce Marshall was published in 1952.

'Wing Commander Yeo-Thomas thus turned his final mission into a success by his determined opposition to the enemy, his strenuous efforts to maintain the morale of his fellow-prisoners and his brilliant escape activities. He endured brutal treatment and torture without flinching and showed the most amazing fortitude and devotion to duty throughout his service abroad, during which he was under the constant threat of death.'
London Gazette

JOHN TRAVERS CORNWELL VC

31 May 1916

Jack Cornwell (1900–16). He grew up in Manor Park, London before leaving school at the age of 14 and working as a delivery boy for a short while before joining the Royal Navy in 1915. A mountain in the Canadian Rockies, a camp for Western Australian Sea Scouts, and a street in Manor Park are all named after him. (IWM, Q 20883)

HMS *Chester* was part of the Grand Fleet commanded by Admiral Sir John Jellicoe at the battle of Jutland. *Chester* was part of the 3rd Battle Cruiser Squadron, and came under withering fire from German ships. Jack Cornwell, aged just 16, was sight-setter for one of the gun crews.

HMS *Chester* was hit by at least 17 150mm shells during the battle. While the ship itself was never in danger of sinking thanks to the captain's skilful seamanship, the men on deck suffered terribly, with around 80 sailors being killed or wounded. Among them was Jack. In the first few minutes of the attack he was mortally wounded. Surrounded by the bodies of his much older comrades, he continued to man the gun alone, quietly awaiting orders. Many of the older sailors took cover from the intense fire, but at no point did Jack leave his post.

When HMS *Chester* retired from the battle, Jack was found still by his gun, shards of steel penetrating his chest. He died of his wounds in hospital two days later. His mother did not get to him in time, and his last words were 'Give my mother my love, I know she is coming.'

He was buried quietly in a public grave, but when his bravery became common knowledge, his mother was persuaded to have him exhumed and reburied in Manor Park Cemetery, east London. Hundreds of people, including boy scouts, lined the route of the cortege, and he was buried with full naval honours. His father was buried in the same grave a month later when he died of bronchitis while on home service.

Cornwell had only joined the Royal Navy the previous year as a Boy First Class and his posting to HMS *Chester*, was his first following training. Admiral Sir David Beatty recommended that Boy Cornwell be awarded the Victoria Cross for his astonishing bravery in the face of devastating enemy fire despite his extreme youth and relative inexperience. He quickly became a symbol of the courageous nature of British youth and there are many memorials to him. The gun he manned is still displayed in the Imperial War Museum.

The artist Frank O. Salisbury painted a portrait of Cromwell at his post on the HMS *Chester*, using his younger brother as a model. Despite his posthumous fame, his family struggled financially after the First World War, and most of his siblings were forced to emigrate. (IWM, Q 68247)

JACK WAS THE YOUNGEST VICTORIA CROSS RECIPIENT IN THE FIRST WORLD WAR.

APPENDICES

Private John Freeman VC
1857, India, 9th Lancers

Colour Sergeant William Gardner VC
1858, India, 42nd Regiment

Sergeant Albert Gill VC
1916, France, 1st Battalion, King's Royal Rifle Corps

Driver Horace Glasock VC
1900, South Africa, Q Battery, Royal Horse Artillery

Lieutenant Robert Gorle VC
1918, Belgium, 50th Brigade, Royal Field Artillery

Major Charles Gough VC
1857–1858, India, 5th Bengal European Cavalry

Corporal John Grimshaw VC
1915, Turkey, 1st Battalion, Lancashire Fusiliers

Major John Guise VC
1857, India, 90th Regiment

Midshipman Basil Guy VC, RN
1900, China, Naval Brigade

Lieutenant Thomas Hackett VC
1857, India, 23rd Regiment

Lieutenant Walter Hamilton VC
1879, Afghanistan, Queen's Own Corps of Guides

Captain Arthur Hammond VC
1879, Afghanistan, Queen's Own Corps of Guides

Gunner Israel Harding VC
1882, Egypt, HMS *Alexandra*

Lieutenant Reginald Hart VC
1879, Afghanistan, Royal Engineers

Private Jack Harvey VC
1918, France, 1/22nd Battalion, London Regiment

Captain Arthur Henderson VC
1917, France, 2nd Battalion, Argyll and Sutherland
Highlanders

Lieutenant Colonel Edward Henderson VC
1917, Mesopotamia, 9th Battalion, Royal Warwickshire
Regiment

Captain Alexander Hore-Ruthven VC
1898, Sudan, 3rd Battalion, Highland Light Infantry

Lieutenant Alec Horwood VC
1944, Burma, 1st Battalion, Northamptonshire Regiment

Sepoy Ishar Singh VC
1921, India, 28th Punjab Regiment

Sergeant Norman Jackson VC
1944, Germany, 106 Squadron, RAF

Captain Manley James VC
1918, France, 8th Battalion, Gloucestershire Regiment

Private Robert Jones VC
1879, South Africa, 2nd Battalion, 24th Regiment

Sepoy Kamal Ram VC
1944, Italy, 3rd Battalion, 8th Punjab Regiment

Private Henry Kenny VC
1915, France, 1st Battalion, Loyal North Lancashire
Regiment

Lieutenant William Kenny VC
1920, India, 4/39th Garhwal Rifles

Lieutenant Allan Ker VC
1918, France, 61st Battalion, Machine Gun Corps

Captain William Kerr VC
1857, India, 24th Bombay Native Infantry

Lieutenant Colonel Geoffrey Keyes VC
1941, Libya, Royal Scots Greys (No.11 Scottish
Commando)

Corporal Frank Kirby VC
1900, South Africa, Royal Engineers

Sergeant Tom Lawrence VC
1900, South Africa, 17th Lancers

2nd Lieutenant James Leach VC
1914, France, 2nd Battalion, Manchester Regiment

Flight Lieutenant Roderick Learoyd VC
1940, Germany, 49 Squadron, RAF

Private Frank Lester VC
1918, France, 10th Battalion, Lancashire Fusiliers

Private Hubert Lewis VC
1916, Greece, 11th Battalion, Welsh Regiment

Captain Aidan Liddell VC
1915, Belgium, 7 Squadron, RFC

Commander John Linton VC RN
1939-43, Mediterranean, HM Submarine *Turbulent*

Sergeant Joseph Lister VC
1917, Belgium, 1st Battalion, Lancashire Fusiliers

Flight Lieutenant David Lord VC
1944, Holland, 271 Squadron, RAF

Major Stewart Loudoun-Shand VC
1916, France, 10th Battalion, Yorkshire Regiment

Driver Frederick Luke VC
1914, France, 37th Battery, Royal Field Artillery

Lieutenant Harry Lyster VC
1858, India, 72nd Bengal Native Infantry

Lieutenant Hector Maclean VC
1897, India, Queen's Own Corps of Guides

Seaman James Magennis VC
1945, Singapore, HM Midget Submarine *XE 3*

Surgeon William Maillard VC RN
1898, Crete, HMS *Hazard*

Midshipman Wilfred Malleson VC RN
1915, Turkey, SS *River Clyde*

Major Edward Mannock VC
1918, France, 85 Squadron, RAF

Flying Officer Leslie Manser VC
1942, Germany, 50 Squadron, RAF

Lieutenant Percival Marling VC
1884, Sudan, 3rd Battalion, King's Royal Rifle Corps

Sergeant Horace Martineau VC
1899, South Africa, Protectorate Regiment

Lieutenant Francis Maxwell VC
1900, South Africa, 18th Bengal Lancers

Surgeon John McCrea VC
1881, Basutoland, 1st Cape Mounted Yeomanry

William McDonell VC
1857, India, Bengal Civil Service

Sergeant Samuel McGaw VC
1874, Ashanti, 42nd Regiment

Private George McIntosh VC
1917, Belgium, 1/6th Battalion, Gordon Highlanders

Sergeant Ian McKay VC
1982, Falkland Islands, 3rd Battalion, Parachute Regiment

Sergeant William McNally VC
1918, Italy, 8th Battalion, Yorkshire Regiment

Lieutenant Colonel John McNeill VC
1864, New Zealand, 107th Regiment (Bengal Infantry)

Commander Anthony Miers VC RN
1942, Mediterranean, HM Submarine *Torbay*

Private Francis Miles VC
1918, France, 1/5th Battalion, Gloucestershire Regiment

Lieutenant Frederick Miller VC
1854, Russia, Royal Artillery

Private Martin Moffat VC
1918, Belgium, 2nd Battalion, Leinster Regiment

Sergeant Thomas Mottershead VC
1917, Belgium, 20 Squadron, RFC

Private Robert Newell VC
1858, India, 9th Lancers

Lieutenant Colonel Augustus Charles Newman VC
1942, France, Essex Regiment (No 2 Commando)

Captain Gerald O'Sullivan VC
1915, Turkey, 1st Battalion, Royal Inniskilling Fusiliers

Private George Peachment VC
1915, France, 2nd Battalion, King's Royal Rifle Corps

Private John Pearson VC
1858, India, 8th Hussars

Captain Frederick Peters VC RN
1942, Algeria, HMS *Walney*

Ensign Everard Phillipps VC
1857, India, 11th Bengal Native Infantry

Lieutenant Arthur Pickard VC
1863, New Zealand, Royal Artillery

Petty Officer Ernest Pitcher VC
1917, Atlantic Ocean, HMS *Dunraven*

Chief Petty Officer George Prowse VC
1918, France, Drake Battalion

Trooper Horace Ramsden VC
1899, South Africa, Protectorate Regiment

Private John Readitt VC
1917, Mesopotamia, 6th Battalion, South Lancashire Regiment

Captain Hamilton Reed VC
1899, South Africa, 7th Battery, Royal Field Artillery

Seaman Thomas Reeves VC
1854, Russia, Naval Brigade

Lieutenant William Rhodes-Moorhouse VC
1915, Belgium, 2 Squadron, RFC

Sergeant Alfred Richards VC
1915, Turkey, 1st Battalion, Lancashire Fusiliers

Quartermaster William Rickard VC
1855, Russia, HMS *Weser*

Lieutenant Peter Roberts VC RN
1942, Mediterranean, HM Submarine *Thrasher*

Lieutenant William Leefe Robinson VC
1916, United Kingdom, 39 Squadron, RFC

Captain George Rolland VC
1903, Somaliland, 1st Bombay Grenadiers

Leading Seaman George Samson VC
1915, Turkey, SS *River Clyde*

Captain Harry Schofield VC
1899, South Africa, Royal Field Artillery

Seaman Mark Scholefield VC
1854, Russia, Naval Brigade

Naik Shahamad Khan VC
1916, Mesopotamia, 89th Punjab Regiment

Corporal John Shaul VC
1899, South Africa, 1st Battalion, Highland Light Infantry

Lance Sergeant Edward Smith VC
1918, France, 1/5th Battalion, Lancashire Fusiliers

Captain Frederick Smith VC
1864, New Zealand, 43rd Regiment

Sergeant Quentin Smythe VC
1942, Libya, Royal Natal Carabineers

Sergeant Thomas Steele VC
1917, Mesopotamia, 1st Battalion, Seaforth Highlanders

Flying Officer Lloyd Trigg VC
1943, Atlantic Ocean, 200 Squadron, RAF (RNZAF)

Lieutenant William Waller VC
1858, India, 25th Bombay Light Infantry

Lieutenant Tasker Watkins VC
1944, France, 1/5th Battalion, Welch Regiment

Lieutenant John Watson VC
1857, India, 1st Punjab Cavalry

2nd Lieutenant Frank Wearne VC
1917, France, 11th Battalion, Essex Regiment

Lieutenant Colonel Richard West VC
1918, France, 6th Battalion, Tank Corps

Captain Harry Whitchurch VC
1895, India, Indian Medical Service

2nd Lieutenant William White VC
1918, France, 38th Battalion, Machine Gun Corps

Lance-Corporal Alfred Wilcox VC
1918, France, 2/4th Battalion, Oxford and Buckinghamshire Light Infantry

Private Alfred Wilkinson VC
1918, France, 1/5th Battalion, Manchester Regiment

Able Seaman William Williams VC
1915, Turkey, SS *River Clyde*

Captain Eric Wilson VC
1940, Somaliland, East Surrey Regiment, attached Somali Mounted Infantry

Lieutenant Sidney Clayton Woodroffe VC
1915, Belgium, 8th Battalion, Rifle Brigade

2nd Lieutenant John Youll VC
1918, Italy, 11th Battalion, Northumberland Fusiliers

Sergeant Major Alexander Young VC
1901, South Africa, Cape Police

VICTORIA CROSSES IN THE IMPERIAL WAR MUSEUM COLLECTION

Lieutenant Augustine Agar VC RN
1919, Russia, HM *Coastal Motor Boat 4*

Lieutenant Colonel William Anderson VC
1918, France, 12th Battalion, Highland Light Infantry

2nd Lieutenant Edward Baxter VC
1916, France, 1/8th Battalion, King's (Liverpool Regiment)

Lieutenant Commander Stephen Beattie VC RN
1942, France, HMS *Campbeltown*

Private Johnson Beharry VC
2004, Iraq, 1st Battalion, Princess of Wales's Royal Regiment

Captain Edward Bradbury VC
1914, France, L Battery, Royal Horse Artillery

Sergeant William Burman VC
1917, Belgium, 16th Battalion, Rifle Brigade

Captain Alfred Carpenter VC RN
1918, Belgium, HMS *Vindictive*

Private George Cartwright VC
1918, France, 33rd (New South Wales) Battalion, AIF

Wing Commander Leonard Cheshire VC
1940–1944, Europe, RAF Volunteer Reserve

Boy First Class Jack Cornwell VC
1916, Jutland, HMS *Chester*

Private Christopher Cox VC
1917, France, 7th Battalion, Bedfordshire Regiment

Corporal John Cunningham VC
1917, France, 2nd Battalion, Leinster Regiment

Corporal John Davies VC
1918, France 11th Battalion, South Lancashire Regiment

Battery Sergeant Major George Dorrell VC
1914, France, L Battery, Royal Horse Artillery

Midshipman George Drewry VC RNR
1915, Turkey, SS *River Clyde*

Lieutenant Commander Eugene Esmonde VC RN
1942, Straits of Dover, 825 Squadron, Fleet Air Arm

Company Sergeant Major George Evans VC
1916, France, 18th Battalion, Manchester Regiment

Lieutenant Gordon Flowerdew VC
1918, France, Lord Strathcona's Horse, CEF

Captain Philip Gardner VC
1941, Libya, 4th Royal Tank Regiment

Corporal Charles Garforth VC
1914, Belgium and France, 15th Hussars

2nd Lieutenant Reginald Haine VC
1917, France, 1st Battalion, Honourable Artillery
Company

Captain Percy Hansen VC
1915, Turkey, 6th Battalion, Lincolnshire Regiment

Lance Corporal William Hewitt VC
1917, Belgium 2nd South African Light Infantry

Able Seaman Albert McKenzie VC
1918, Belgium, HMS Vindictive

Corporal James McPhie VC
1918, France, 416th Field Company, Royal Engineers

Lance Corporal Harold Mugford VC
1917, France, 8th Squadron, Machine Gun Corps

Captain Charles Mullins VC
1899, South Africa, Imperial Light Horse (Natal)

Lieutenant Philip Neame VC
1914, France, 15th Field Company, Royal Engineers

Sergeant David Nelson VC
1914, France, L Battery, Royal Horse Artillery

2nd Lieutenant John Norwood VC
1899, South Africa, 5th Dragoon Guards

Havildar Parkash Singh VC
1943, Burma, 5th Battalion, 8th Punjab Regiment

Lieutenant Godfrey Place VC RN
1943, Norway, HM Midget Submarine X-7

Private Frederick Potts VC
1915, Turkey, 1/1st Berkshire Yeomanry

Captain John Randle VC
1944, Burma, 2nd Battalion, Royal Norfolk Regiment

Private William Ratcliffe VC
1917, Belgium, 2nd Battalion, South Lancashire Regiment

Commander Robert Ryder VC RN
1942, France, HMS Campbeltown

Private Robert Ryder VC
1916, France 12th Battalion, Middlesex Regiment

Lieutenant Colonel Derek Seagrim VC
1943, Tunisia, 7th Battalion, Green Howards

Lieutenant John Smyth VC
1915, France, 15th Ludhiana Sikhs

Commander Edward Unwin VC RN
1915, Turkey, SS River Clyde

Captain Frederick West VC
1918, France, 8 Squadron, RAF

Lieutenant Thomas Wilkinson VC
1916, France, 7th Battalion, Loyal North Lancashire
Regiment

Lieutenant Thomas Wilkinson VC RNR
1942, Java Sea, HMS Li Wo

Lance-Sergeant Joseph Woodall VC
1918, France, 1st Battalion, Rifle Brigade

GEORGE CROSSES IN THE IMPERIAL WAR MUSEUM COLLECTION

Thomas Alderson GC
1940, United Kingdom, ARP Rescue Parties

Lieutenant Selby Armitage GC RNVR
1940, United Kingdom, HMS Vernon

Doreen Ashburnham GC
1916, Canada, child

Sub Lieutenant John Babington GC RNVR
1940, United Kingdom, Royal Naval Volunteer Reserve

Major Herbert Barefoot GC
1940, United Kingdom, No 4 Bomb Disposal Company,
Royal Engineers

Gordon Bastian GC
1943, Atlantic Ocean, SS Empire Bowman

Private Richard Blackburn GC
1935, India, 1st Battalion, Cheshire Regiment

Lieutenant John Bridge GC RNVR
1943, Sicily, Royal Naval Volunteer Reserve

Sub-Lieutenant Francis Brooke-Smith GC RNR
1940–41, United Kingdom, Royal Naval Reserve

Lance Corporal Matthew Croucher GC
2008, Afghanistan, 40 Commando, Royal Marines

Lieutenant Robert Davies GC
1940, United Kingdom, Royal Engineers

Captain Mahmood Durrani GC
1942–1945, Malaya, 1st Bahawalpur Infantry

Chief Petty Officer Reginald Ellingworth GC RN
1940, United Kingdom, HMS Vernon

Private Ernest Elston GC
1935, India, 1st Battalion, West Yorkshire
Regiment

PC Anthony Gledhill GC
1966, United Kingdom, Metropolitan Police

Cadet David Hay GC
1941, Atlantic Ocean, SS Eurylochus

Boatswain William McCarthy GC
1943, Libya, HMS Nile

Lieutenant Harold Newgass GC RNVR
1940, United Kingdom, Royal Naval Volunteer Reserve

Colonel Lanceray Newnham GC
1943, Hong Kong, Middlesex Regiment

Corporal Daphne Pearson GC
1940, United Kingdom, WAAF

Sydney Purvis GC
1929, United Kingdom, Miner

Flight Lieutenant John Quinton GC
1951, United Kingdom, 228 Operational Conversion Unit,
RAF

Lieutenant Edward Reynolds GC
1940, United Kingdom, Nos 101 & 102 Bomb Disposal
Sections, Royal Engineers

Superintendent Gerald Richardson GC
1971, United Kingdom, Lancashire Constabulary

Odette Sansom GC
1942–1945, France, Women's Transport Service (Special
Operations Executive)

Major Hugh Seagrim GC
1944, Burma, 19th Hyderabad Regiment (Force 136)

Wing Commander Laurence Sinclair GC
1940, United Kingdom, 110 Squadron, RAF

Major George Styles GC
1971, United Kingdom, Royal Army Ordnance Corps

Robert Taylor GC
1950, United Kingdom, Civilian

Harry Wilson GC
1924, United Kingdom, Miner

Wing Commander Forest Yeo-Thomas GC
1943–1945, France, Royal Air Force Volunteer Reserve
(Special Operations Executive)